TWEEN SERIES NANCY DREW #11

"SPYING, WEREN'T YOU?", COLLEEN SAID
ACCUSINGLY——

he Clue of the Broken Locket

"WHO ARE YOU?" A WOMAN'S VOICE
DEMANDED SHARPLY.

The Clue of the Broken Locket

"SHE IS THE THIEF!" THE MAN CRIED TRIUMPHANTLY.

The Clue of the Broken Locket   *Frontispiece (Page 197).*

NANCY DREW MYSTERY STORIES

THE CLUE OF THE
BROKEN LOCKET

BY

CAROLYN KEENE

AUTHOR OF THE MYSTERY AT LILAC INN,
THE PASSWORD TO LARKSPUR LANE,
THE CLUE IN THE DIARY, ETC.

ILLUSTRATED BY
RUSSELL H. TANDY

FACSIMILE EDITION

BEDFORD, MASSACHUSETTS
APPLEWOOD BOOKS

For further information about these editions, please write: Applewood Books, Box 365, Bedford, MA 01730.

LIBRARY OF CONGRESS CATALOGING-IN-PUBLICATION DATA
Keene, Carolyn.
    The Clue of the broken locket / by Carolyn Keene; illustrated by Russell H. Tandy. —Facsim. ed.
        p.   cm.   —(Nancy Drew mystery stories)
        Summary: Nancy's sympathy for a pair of adopted twin babies leads her into a surprising mystery.
        ISBN 1-55709-165-X
        [1. Mystery and detective stories.]   I. Tandy, Russell H., ill.   II. Title.   III. Series: Keene, Carolyn. Nancy Drew mystery stories.
PZ7.K23Cn   1998
[Fic]—dc21   98-33891
                                        CIP
                                         AC

10 9 8 7 6 5 4 3 2

PUBLISHER'S NOTE

Much has changed in America since the Nancy Drew series first began in 1930. The modern reader may be delighted with the warmth and exactness of the language, the wholesome innocence of the characters, their engagement with the natural world, or the nonstop action without the use of violence; but just as well, the modern reader may be extremely uncomfortable with the racial and social stereotyping, the roles women play in these books, or the use of phrases or situations which may conjure up some response in the modern reader that was not felt by the reader of the times.

For good or bad, we Americans have changed quite a bit since these books were first issued. Many readers will remember these editions with great affection and will be delighted with their return; others will wonder why we just don't let them disappear. These books are part of our heritage. They are a window on our real past. For that reason, except for the addition of this note, we are presenting *The Clue of the Broken Locket* unedited and unchanged from its first edition.

Applewood Books

NANCY DREW MYSTERY STORIES

THE CLUE OF THE BROKEN LOCKET

BY

CAROLYN KEENE

Author of THE MYSTERY AT LILAC INN,
THE PASSWORD TO LARKSPUR LANE,
THE CLUE IN THE DIARY, ETC.

ILLUSTRATED BY

RUSSELL H. TANDY

NEW YORK

GROSSET & DUNLAP

PUBLISHERS

Made in the United States of America

NANCY DREW
MYSTERY STORIES
By CAROLYN KEENE
12mo. Cloth. Illustrated.

GROSSET & DUNLAP, PUBLISHERS, NEW YORK

CONTENTS

Contents

THE CLUE OF THE BROKEN LOCKET

CHAPTER I

AN ADOPTION

A GRACEFUL young girl, her golden hair flying in the breeze, raced up the back steps of the Drew home and burst into the kitchen.

She shut the door with a bang which caused Hannah Gruen, the middle-aged housekeeper, to drop a pan.

"My goodness, Nancy!" she exclaimed. "You're enough to scare a body out of a year's growth!"

"Sorry," the girl laughed. "I didn't mean to come in like a cyclone, but it's Saturday; and on Saturday I always feel especially well."

"Saturday and Sunday and all the rest of the days," Hannah retorted. "But I wish your father had some of your spirit today. I declare, I believe he is working too hard."

Nancy's face grew thoughtful.

1

"Dad didn't look very cheerful at breakfast this morning," she reflected.

"And I made hot cakes especially for him," the kind-hearted housekeeper continued in a slightly aggrieved tone. "Did you notice anything wrong?"

"Wrong? Well, since you mention it, I did. He seemed preoccupied."

"Oh, I mean about the hot cakes. Did they taste all right to you?"

Nancy laughed.

"They were delicious. Don't worry about your cooking, for you're the best cook in River Heights. I'm sure Dad won't be able to resist that creamed chicken you're preparing for luncheon."

Hannah beamed as she went over to the stove to stir the savory mixture which was bubbling in a gleaming pan.

"I'm ready to put the things on the table now," she announced as Nancy went into the adjoining room. "You might call your father."

Carson Drew appeared to be reading a newspaper in the living room, but on closer inspection Nancy observed him merely to be staring at it. He did not hear her approaching, and it was not until she spoke that he looked up.

"Why, hello, Nancy. How is my little girl today?"

"You asked me that question this morning at breakfast."

"So I did," the lawyer smiled. "I—I seem to be rather absent-minded today."

Nancy cast a troubled glance at her father's drawn face. Something was wrong; of that she was certain. She did not wish to annoy him with questions just yet, so announced luncheon instead. Together they entered the dining room.

"I'm half starved!" she declared as Hannah brought in the steaming dishes. Then, turning to her father, she inquired, "Did you have a hard morning at court?"

"Not more so than usual."

Nancy made several attempts at casual conversation, but met with no success. Her father seemed completely absorbed in his own thoughts, and for the most part did not follow the trend of what she was saying. He toyed with his food, eating even less than he had at breakfast.

"Dad, you're worrying about something," she said abruptly when the kitchen door had closed. "If it's about finances I wish you'd tell me."

Carson Drew raised his eyes from his plate, and smiled.

"I'm not worrying about money matters, Nancy."

"Well, if it isn't finances, it must be a law case!"

"I see you have me on the witness stand,

Nancy, so I may as well confess I am worried over that very thing, and a most peculiar case at that.''

The girl's blue eyes shone with interest.

"Tell me about it. You recall you promised me once that I might be your partner!"

"In all matters of mystery," Mr. Drew answered. "This isn't exactly that type of case, although it does have a mysterious angle to it."

"Mysterious angles are my specialty."

"I fear there's nothing you can do to help me this time, Nancy. It's an adoption case. I wish now I had turned it down. But when Mr. and Mrs. Blair first called at my office they appeared to be good people."

"Didn't I see them there Tuesday?"

"Perhaps you did. Kitty Blair is a fairly well-known singer and her husband does specialty dances. I've met a great many actors and actresses in my time, all of them mighty fine people—but these Blairs, well, I can't make them out."

"I must say I didn't like their looks myself."

"They strike me as being unstable, with a flair for the limelight and publicity. I don't like to think of their being the parents of such fine babies as Jay and Janet."

"You're talking in riddles!" Nancy exclaimed. "Do you mean the Blairs are adopting children?"

"Yes, twins from the Foundling Home at

Selkirk. They go by the names of Jay and Janet.''

"What's the mysterious angle?" asked Nancy.

"The babies were found under rather strange circumstances. I can't recall the details now. However, I do know that some fine clothing and a strange sort of locket were found with the babies.''

"Evidence that their parents must have had money," Nancy said musingly.

"It would seem so. The twins are of unusual intelligence, too, the matron of the Home tells me.''

"Don't you think that if she has the babies' welfare at heart, she should refuse to allow the Blairs to adopt them?''

"She has been hoodwinked by their gushing manner and their money," Mr. Drew informed her. "Unfortunately, she has given her consent and signed the papers.''

"Isn't there anything you can do to prevent the adoption?''

Mr. Drew shook his head regretfully.

"I fear not. I have tried to discourage the Blairs but they seem determined. I must confess I have nothing in particular against them. They simply strike me as frivolous people.''

"They may change their minds before the papers are signed," Nancy said hopefully.

"It isn't likely. They are coming here this

afternoon to arrange the final details before taking the children from the Home. Perhaps I am worrying unnecessarily, but I wish I didn't have to go through with the thing.''

"You aren't exactly responsible," Nancy declared, "yet I know how you feel. I wish something could be done.''

"Now, don't worry your pretty head about this affair, Nancy. I shouldn't have told you, because I know you are inclined to involve yourself in other people's troubles.''

"I guess there's nothing I can do this time," Nancy confessed. "But if you don't mind, I should like to meet the prospective parents when they come here today.''

"Speak to them if you like, though I fear you'll find them very shallow.''

At that moment the doorbell rang. Presently Hannah appeared, saying that Mr. and Mrs. Blair were in the living room.

"They're quarreling about something," the housekeeper added in a whisper to Nancy. "Nice folks, I must say!''

The Blairs were talking so loudly that their voices carried to the dining room. It was impossible not to hear what they were saying.

"I'll never agree to call the babies Jay and Janet!" the woman proclaimed. "Never! I want nothing to remind me of their past. Do you hear, Johnny?''

"I'm not deaf," was the sarcastic retort.

"Pipe down! We'll settle about names later—and other things as well."

The argument was cut short as Carson Drew entered the living room.

"Mrs. Blair, this is my daughter, Nancy."

"Kitty Blair, if you don't mind," the actress corrected, her voice changing to a soft purr. "You must have heard of me, Miss Drew. I had the leading rôle in the Century Follies."

"Oh, yes," Nancy murmured, and turned to acknowledge Mr. Blair's greeting.

"Pleased to meet you," he grinned.

Mr. Drew excused himself, and went into his study for the adoption papers which the Blairs had come to sign.

Alone with the two visitors, Nancy studied them closely without appearing to do so. Her worst fears were confirmed.

Kitty Blair was over-rouged and over-dressed. Her bearing was proud and haughty, her gestures dramatic. Her voice had a hard, metallic ring, except when she tried to be particularly agreeable. It was clear to Nancy that the actress considered herself very important.

In appearance, Johnny Blair was very ordinary. His face was almost expressionless. He was several inches shorter than his wife and seemed dominated by her.

"My father tells me that you are adopting little Jay and Janet," Nancy commented as an aid to conversation. "They are adorable babies. It seems a shame their parents have never claimed them."

"Humph!" Kitty Blair's green eyes flashed. "When a mother abandons her children, she should lose all right to them!"

"Perhaps she didn't actually abandon them," Nancy countered. "She may have been in some sort of an accident which brought about the separation and now cannot locate them. Or, she may have been parted from them by some very, very strange trick of fate."

"Then that was her misfortune," the actress responded tartly.

"Isn't it true that the twins were found under rather unusual circumstances?" Nancy probed.

"I didn't trouble to find out," the actress replied indifferently. "The matron showed me a bundle of clothes and a broken locket which she said had been picked up near the place where the children were first seen. I'll dispose of everything as soon as the package is turned over to me."

"Oh, you mustn't do that!" Nancy cried involuntarily. "If you do, the only existing clue to the babies' parentage will be lost."

"And that will suit me fine! I'll not have any parents turning up in a few years to claim the youngsters."

"Your adoption papers would give you the prior claim, I believe," Nancy told her. "But if the real parents should be located, it would be cruel never to let them see the children.''

"The twins must be reared as our own flesh and blood," Mrs. Blair insisted. "After we sign the adoption papers, no one else has any rights at all in the case.''

"But the babies surely have the privilege of knowing their own mother and father," Nancy protested.

"They'll be better off if they never find out a thing about 'em," Johnny Blair broke in. "We'll raise 'em as stage kids should be raised. By the time they're ten or twelve, they'll be dragging in good money. Twins should be a sensation behind footlights.''

Mr. Drew returned to the living room with the papers which were ready for the Blairs' signatures. Reluctantly, he indicated where they were to sign their names.

"Your real name is Sellenstein, I believe," he said politely.

"We don't use it any more," Johnny Blair informed the lawyer.

"Nevertheless, it will be best to sign the papers that way.''

Kitty scowled, but did as she was requested. Johnny wrote his name with a grand flourish.

"Now the twins are really ours!" the actress announced with satisfaction. "We can do just as we please with them and no one has any legal right to interfere.''

"You must remember that you are accepting a grave responsibility," the attorney said quietly.

The actress pretended not to hear him.

"Come, Johnny," she commanded. "We'll drive straight to the Home now and get the twins. I guess the Dunbars will be surprised when they come to our party tonight!"

"The Dunbars," Mr. Drew echoed.

"Theatrical friends of ours," Mr. Blair explained. "They have a kid of their own they're raising for the stage, and they like to keep rubbing it in that we have no children. Guess our twins will make them quiet down for a while!"

Mr. Drew accompanied the Blairs to the door. When he returned to the living room, he found Nancy slumped down in an upholstered chair.

"Oh, Dad, it's awful!" she said. "I don't wonder you feel almost ill."

"I'm afraid they mean to exploit the babies," Mr. Drew remarked slowly.

"I'm certain of it! I stood there wishing and hoping that something would prevent the Blairs from signing those papers."

"So did I. But it's over now."

Nancy nodded despondently.

"Mrs. Blair means to destroy all evidence regarding the parentage of the children, too. *We must prevent that.*"

"There's nothing we can do."

The lawyer sat down wearily on the divan.

The day had been extremely trying for him. Nancy knew that he was distressed, and decided to say no more concerning the adoption for the time being.

However, a firm resolve was shaping itself in her mind. She was determined that the Blairs should not destroy the bundle of baby clothing and the broken locket!

"I must act quickly, or it will be too late," she thought. "I don't dare to drop a hint to Father, for he'll caution me against interfering."

While Nancy was standing by the window thinking, she heard the doorbell ring again. Wondering if the Blairs had returned, Mr. Drew went to answer it. He returned with a telegram in his hand.

Nancy took slight notice of the envelope, for her father often received such messages at his home regarding matters of business routine. However, at a sharp exclamation from him she glanced up.

"What is it, Father? Not bad news, I hope."

Without answering, Mr. Drew offered her the telegram. It read:

DO NOT LET THE BLAIRS ADOPT MY BABIES

The message was signed "Broken Heart."

CHAPTER II

The Broken Locket

"If this message had arrived fifteen minutes earlier I might have delayed the adoption," Mr. Drew said regretfully. "I usually take no stock in anonymous communications, but this one is somehow different."

Nancy thoughtfully fingered the missive.

"The mother of the twins must have sent this, for she speaks of them as 'my babies,'" she said.

"Yes, and moreover she signs herself 'Broken Heart,'" returned her father. "No doubt she will be distressed to learn that it is too late to prevent the adoption."

"It seems to me that this telegram proves a number of things," mused Nancy. "First, that the mother is alive. She is really interested in the welfare of her babies, and in some manner has kept in touch with the Home."

Mr. Drew nodded.

"Otherwise, she couldn't have known that the Blairs were about to adopt the twins," he replied. "Oh, it's a shame! And my hands are tied."

"Mine aren't," Nancy said quickly. "I realize that your position makes it impossible for you to take an active part in the matter, but I mean to interest myself in the case."

"Just what can you do, Nancy?"

"For one thing, I believe I can prevent Mrs. Blair from destroying all evidence concerning the babies' parentage."

"That may not be easy. You can't force her to give up the bundle."

"Perhaps not, but there are other ways. I can't tell you about it now, but I have a plan I think will work!"

Delaying only long enough to obtain the address of the Blair estate, which was located about fifteen miles from River Heights, Nancy hurried to the garage. Her own shiny new automobile stood waiting for her, ready for just such an adventure as she now expected to undertake.

The energetic girl was adept at handling the car, and guided it skillfully down the drive in reverse gear. Often Hannah Gruen would shudder as she watched her mistress, predicting that Nancy would some day come into collision with the big oak tree near the curb. However, it was Carson Drew who, while driving, had pulled a large-sized strip of bark from the trunk. The fenders of Nancy's cars had never so much as been scratched.

Intent upon her visit to Jolly Folly, the

Blairs' pretentious estate, the girl drove at a careful speed down the street. She paused at a red traffic light, and was looking impatiently at it when she heard her name called.

"Hello, Nancy Drew!"

"Hello, Bess Marvin!" Nancy cried, swinging open the door. "Jump in, and I'll give you a lift."

"But I'm going the other way."

"Then I'll give you a long ride as well as an adventure!"

Bess could not resist such a tempting suggestion, particularly since she had no plans for the afternoon. When Nancy promised excitement, she always kept her word.

Quickly Bess slipped into the seat, and they drove off.

"What's this about an adventure?" she demanded. "Don't tell me you've dug up another mystery, Nancy."

"I don't know yet whether it's a mystery or not, but there's plenty of chance for good detective work," Nancy chuckled.

Bess listened attentively to the story of the adoption of little Jay and Janet, and promptly agreed that she would drive to Jolly Folly with her chum.

"Nancy, you're the most amazing girl in the world. How you can ferret out so much excitement is beyond me!"

Nancy always had been a source of wonder

to her friends. She had a natural genius for solving mysteries, as her father had discovered. He enjoyed discussing his interesting law cases with her, and found her opinions to be astonishingly sound for one so young.

Left motherless at an early age, Nancy had developed a fine sense of responsibility and more than earned her right to complete freedom. She had a keen mind, a quick sympathy for those in trouble, and an ability to look out for herself.

A fine old timepiece on the mantel in her home served to remind Nancy of her first exciting mystery. Her encounter with the Tophams is revealed in "The Secret of the Old Clock," the first volume of the series.

Other adventures followed in quick succession, once her reputation as a detective was established. A queer bungalow, an old ranch, and even a farm provided scenes for her triumphs.

Nancy's eyes became sharpened to clues which others failed to notice, as was the case in "The Password to Larkspur Lane." There a carrier pigeon led her to a mysterious retreat, where the girl brought about the release of a sweet old lady being held against her wishes.

Well acquainted with her chum's prowess, Bess Marvin was convinced that Nancy could evolve excitement from anything. She saw the making of a splendid adventure in their dash to Jolly Folly to prevent Mrs. Blair from destroying the bundle of clothing and the broken locket.

Nancy was not thinking of the trip in such terms. Her sole purpose was to aid the helpless little twins and possibly the distressed mother, who had signed herself "Broken Heart."

Nancy was puzzling over the queer message, when she rounded a curve and observed a large touring car stalled at the edge of the pavement. As she slowed down, a man stepped out and motioned for her to halt.

"I've run out of gas," he said in a loud voice. "My wife and I were on our way to the Blair estate. Could you give us a lift?"

The man was well dressed, but his manner, though not offensive, was noticeably crude. The girls caught a glimpse of a woman and a pretty child seated in the stalled automobile.

It was in Nancy's nature to want to be of assistance; in this instance, the man's request fitted in perfectly with her plans.

"By all means ride with us," she invited. "My route carries me directly toward the Blair estate."

"My name is Dunbar," the man introduced himself. "Phil Dunbar."

"I believe I've heard Mr. and Mrs. Blair speak of you," Nancy commented.

"Then you know them?"

"Only slightly. In fact, I have met them but once."

"Phil," came the woman's voice from the car, "what is all the delay for? If they won't take us free of charge, offer them money."

Directing an apologetic glance toward Nancy and Bess, Phil Dunbar hurried to his wife's side to acquaint her with the situation. She came back with him, leading an unwilling little girl by the hand.

"I don't want to go!" the child screamed. "I don't want to go!"

"Such a silly, spoiled child!" Nancy thought to herself.

"Mitzi has a will of her own," Mrs. Dunbar smiled. "She has my temperament."

Mr. Dunbar introduced his wife as "Boots." She would have gone into a lengthy account of their exploits on the stage had Nancy not cut her short by saying that she was in a great hurry.

"But where are we to ride?" Mrs. Dunbar asked, gazing askance at the rumble-seat.

"I'll ride back there," Bess offered generously. "I don't mind it in the least."

Mrs. Dunbar did not protest at such a sacrifice. She deposited herself beside Nancy, the child between them. Bess and Phil Dunbar shared the rumble seat.

During the ride Mrs. Dunbar grew talkative. She explained to Nancy that she and her husband were going to the Blair estate to help celebrate the adoption of a baby.

"She'll be surprised when she learns there are twins," thought the girl.

Nancy offered scant information of her own. Instead, she adroitly drew from Mrs. Dunbar many interesting facts concerning the Blairs. The woman intimated that they lived beyond their means, that they were not as famous as they would have people believe, and that their one ambition was to create a great name for themselves.

Nancy gathered from all this palaver that the two actresses were jealous rivals beneath the guise of friendship.

"Imagine Kitty with a child of her own!" Mrs. Dunbar rattled on. "What a joke! She hasn't the least bit of maternal instinct, you know. Now, I'm supremely devoted to my Mitzi!"

"Perhaps," Nancy commented inwardly.

She realized that the Dunbars and the Blairs were far from typical stage people. No doubt they were as much disliked by the members of their profession as they were by strangers. Mitzi, Nancy thought, was a tragic example of what the wrong sort of education will do to a child.

"If the Blairs rear Jay and Janet, they'll grow to be like Mitzi," she reflected.

As they had now reached Jolly Folly, Nancy

turned into the winding gravel drive. The house was a large rambling affair, built by its previous owner. Originally, the estate had been an aristocratic and conservative place. However, in making changes the Blairs had succeeded in flaunting themselves. They had added too many flower beds, gaudy umbrellas and awnings to be in good taste.

Nancy's heart quickened a beat as she observed the Blairs' automobile parked at the front entrance. She did not understand how they could have managed to reach the Selkirk Home, get the babies, and arrive at Jolly Folly ahead of her.

Nancy brought her car to a halt alongside theirs, and as she stepped to the running-board she was relieved to notice that Mrs. Blair and a nursemaid were just alighting.

"They haven't had time to destroy the clothes yet," she told herself.

The Dunbars greeted their friends effusively; in the confusion, Nancy and Bess had an opportunity to look at the twins. The nurse, a pretty young woman, held the children gingerly in her arms, as if she were not yet accustomed to her new duties.

"Oh, aren't they cunning!" Bess cried. "Jay has the sweetest little dimple. Or is it Janet?"

"It's Janet, Miss," the girl responded indifferently. "The only way I can tell 'em apart is by the ribbons. Pink for Janet and blue for Jay.''

Nancy had never before seen such adorable twins. They appeared to be about fourteen months old. At the moment Nancy's eyes were roaming elsewhere, however. For as the maid stepped from the car, a small bundle dropped from her lap and onto the running-board. The girl stood with her back to it, seemingly unaware that it had fallen.

Nancy eyed the package speculatively. The paper wrapping had been torn in one place. She caught a glimpse of something white and lacy.

''Baby clothes,'' she decided. ''The locket must be inside, too. It's the package I want, and I'll get it!''

The Blairs and the Dunbars were absorbed in their conversation, and the nursemaid was talking with Bess. Nancy decided to take a chance. Quickly she reached down, and with a deft movement caught up the bundle and thrust it under her coat.

CHAPTER III

The Bundle of Evidence

Nancy's elation was short-lived.

No sooner had she slipped the bundle beneath her coat than she observed that the Blairs' chauffeur was watching her from the front seat of the car. Had he seen her pick up the package? She could not tell definitely.

Before she could decide what to do, Mrs. Blair turned toward her.

"It was so good of you to bring the Dunbars," she gushed. "You and your friend must stay for our party."

Nancy was on the verge of offering an excuse, but it died in her throat.

"Colleen, carry in the babies," Mrs. Blair ordered, and with an imperious gesture toward the chauffeur, said: "Rodney, gather up the packages we brought from the Home!"

"Yes, Ma'am."

The chauffeur came toward the rear of the automobile where Nancy was standing. He was a tall, thin man, prematurely gray. His eyes were shielded by thick glasses.

"There was another," he said distinctly. "A small one."

21

His gaze wandered toward Nancy. Although he said nothing more, she felt sure that he knew she was holding something under the fold of her coat.

As casually as possible, she offered him the parcel.

"I picked it up on the running-board," she explained. "Is this the one you are looking for?" she asked innocently.

"Don't lose that bundle, Rodney!" Mrs. Blair cut in sharply. "I'm going to burn the things in it tonight! We'll make a grand ceremony of it."

"Not if I can help it," Nancy thought grimly.

Now that she had lost the package, her only course was to remain for the party. As soon as she might have regained the precious baby clothes and the locket, she and Bess could hurry away.

Mrs. Blair escorted her guests into the house. The interior was furnished in flamboyant style, and it seemed to the girls that photographs of theatrical favorites were hung everywhere.

"We'll get away as soon as we can," Nancy promised her chum. "But first I must get that bundle."

Rodney had placed all the packages on the table. The one Nancy wanted was within arm's length of where she was, but she dared not take it when there were so many others in the room.

Realizing that for the time being she must wait, she turned her attention to the twins. The nursemaid permitted them to be handed about from person to person.

To Nancy's horror, Johnny Blair tossed Jay high into the air, catching him as he came down.

"Oh, do be careful!" she pleaded. "If he should fall——"

"Say, I've been catching grown men in tumbling and acrobatic acts for years!"

"But Jay isn't a trained athlete. He's a tiny baby and a fall might cripple him for life."

Mr. Blair laughed boisterously.

"I'm going to toughen this kid up a bit. Six months from now I'll have him turning cartwheels."

Nancy bit her lip and said no more. But she was more than ever determined that the Blairs should never destroy the bundle of evidence. As long as the original baby clothes and the locket remained, there was some hope that the real mother of the twins might be found.

Bess Marvin presently managed to capture the frightened Jay, and held him quietly in her arms. Janet was passed from one person to another, even Mitizi being allowed to carry her about.

Several times Nancy tried to protest, but the guests paid no heed to her warnings. As their conversation grew louder, heightened no doubt by the drinks which Johnny Blair mixed and brought from the sideboard, she arose impatiently.

Brushing past the center table, she deliberately knocked the package of baby garments to the floor. She had hoped that the wrapping would break, which it did. The contents spilled over the floor.

Murmuring an apology for what she termed "a stupid act," Nancy bent down to pick up the things. There were two little handmade white dresses, trimmed with dainty lace and embroidery. Only a loving mother's hand could have fashioned such exquisite garments.

Of far greater interest to Nancy was a curious object which had rolled across the rug. It was a heart-shaped locket. One half of it was missing.

As Nancy stared at the trinket a strange thought flashed through her mind. Could there be any connection between the broken locket and the way the telegram to her father had been signed?

Mrs. Blair was annoyed at the "accident." She beckoned to Colleen.

"Do take those packages upstairs at once. I don't want them cluttering up the living room."

For the second time Nancy saw the baby garments and the locket literally snatched from her grasp. But she had glimpsed them!

Furthermore, she did not intend to leave the house without the bundle.

The party was growing more and more noisy, and additional guests were arriving. Everyone made a great fuss over the twins—fondling and playing with them, and in the estimation of Bess and Nancy, handling them very roughly.

Johnny Blair and Phil Dunbar took turns entertaining with tap dancing to the accompaniment of a blaring radio. Without being asked to do so, Kitty sang several popular songs. Even little Mitzi was called upon to perform.

"She's just like a doll that you wind up to do things mechanically," Bess whispered to her chum. "If the twins grow up to follow in her footsteps, it certainly will be sad."

"Pretty swell kid, eh?" Phil said. "The movies will be picking her up any day now."

"Our twins will make a great sensation when we introduce them on the stage," Kitty declared. "But we must change their stupid, old-fashioned names to something modern."

This was the cue for the guests to suggest what they considered suitable ones and long, heated arguments ensued, as the air grew thick with cigarette smoke, and drinks were passed freely. Nancy and Bess, joining in none of the festivities, were very glad to find themselves ignored. Had it not been for the twins they would have left at once. Yet they lingered, hoping that they might accomplish the mission which had brought them to Jolly Folly.

Jay and Janet were very well-behaved babies, but they did not enjoy being handled by so many strangers. First little Jay began to whimper; then Janet let out a loud wail.

Mrs. Blair was quite helpless in the face of such a situation.

"Oh, someone take them away," she said pettishly. "I can't stand to hear babies cry. What has become of Colleen? Why is she never here when I want her?"

Nancy quickly arose and picked up Janet, wiping away the tears with a handkerchief. Bess went over to Jay and took him in her arms.

"We'll carry them upstairs and put them to bed," Nancy offered.

Mrs. Blair was so busy telling one of the guests about her latest show that she paid scant attention to the girls from River Heights.

No one offered to tell Nancy where she might find the nursery. Accordingly, she and her chum climbed the stairs and opened several doors in search of the room. Finally they discovered it at the end of the hall.

The nursery had been prepared especially for the arrival of the twins. Two small cribs stood by a wall. After quieting the babies, the girls tucked them into their beds.

Not until then did Nancy notice that the careless maid had dropped a number of packages on the floor in the corner of the room. With a cry of delight, she caught up the torn one which contained the baby garments and the locket.

"Let's take the bundle and get away as quickly as we can," Bess advised.

Nancy was examining the baby clothes for marks of identification, but could find none. They reminded her very much of dresses which she, as a child, had put on one of her dolls.

"We can't go downstairs with this bundle, Bess. If we do, the Blairs will ask questions. Kitty is determined to burn these things."

"We mustn't let her do that."

"No. I have an idea! If we could only find a telephone upstairs!"

"I saw one in the hall."

"Then we can do it! I hope Hannah will co-operate with us in our plan."

"What are you talking about?" Bess questioned in bewilderment. "Your mind moves too fast for me to follow."

Nancy chuckled softly.

"This is my idea. I'll exchange these baby clothes for some doll dresses I have packed in the attic at home. Mrs. Blair may burn them for all I care!"

"We have no way to get the things here, Nancy. If we go back for them, Mrs. Blair may destroy the evidence while we're gone."

"That's where Hannah comes in. I'll ask

her to come out in a taxi and bring the little dresses with her.''

"She'll think we're out of our minds!''

"Probably, but that's of no consequence. If she'll just do as we direct! Let's try it, anyway, Bess.''

Quickly, Nancy put in her call. There was a brief wait which seemed endless before the familiar voice of the housekeeper was heard at the other end of the line. As clearly as possible Nancy explained what she wanted her to do.

"Now don't ask questions, Hannah,'' she said hurriedly. "I'll explain everything later. Just get me the white doll clothes in the attic. Oh, yes, and the gold locket I wore as a child! Don't forget the locket, because it's very important.''

"And you want me to come out to Jolly Folly in a taxi?'' the housekeeper demanded incredulously. "I'm right in the midst of my baking.''

"Let it go. You *must* come, Hannah! Please do as I tell you!''

So eager was Nancy to convince the housekeeper of the importance of the trip, that she failed to notice Bess, who was making frantic motions. Not until she hung up the receiver did she realize that anything was amiss.

Kitty Blair had come quietly up a back stairway and was standing scarcely a dozen yards away at the door of the nursery!

CHAPTER IV

NANCY'S STRATEGY

NANCY's heart skipped a beat. From Mrs. Blair's expression she could not tell how much of the conversation had been overheard.

"I was just talking to our housekeeper," she explained easily. "I wanted to tell her where I am. I'll pay you for the call, of course."

"Indeed you'll not," the actress returned grandly. "I am indebted to you for the magnificent way in which you have come to my aid. Really, I had no idea babies could be such a bore!"

"I think it is time for them to be fed," Nancy ventured. "Perhaps you'd like to take charge, Mrs. Blair."

The actress shuddered.

"Oh, dear me, no! Colleen must attend to such things."

"But she seems to have disappeared."

"Then the babies must wait, I fear. I just ran upstairs to change into a tea gown. I haven't time to bother with the twins now."

The girls found it difficult to conceal their disgust.

"Let me assist you," Nancy offered. "It

won't do for them to go without milk at least."

Mrs. Blair looked relieved.

"The cook will give you anything you need, Miss Drew. I can't tell you how sweet it is of you to take such an interest in my babies!"

"Your babies!" Nancy thought. It was truly ironical, to say the least.

Mrs. Blair vanished into her bedroom, but presently emerged, wearing a dazzling red silk tea gown with a long, sweeping train. She stepped into the nursery for a minute to survey herself like a proud peacock before the mirror.

When Nancy and Bess failed to pay her compliments, she seemed somewhat disappointed.

"This gown was designed especially for me," she informed them. "The cost was terrific, but it does flatter my figure, don't you think?"

"Indeed it does," Bess murmured politely.

Nancy said nothing. Mrs. Blair was too taken up with admiring her own reflection to notice the girl's silence.

After the actress had rejoined her boisterous guests, Bess and Nancy went down to the kitchen. There they found the negligent Colleen talking with the cook. Both were in a disgruntled mood.

"I signed up to take care of a baby, not two babies!" they heard Colleen complain. "They'd keep me stepping every minute if I let 'em."

"If jobs weren't so scarce, I'd quit this place," the cook rejoined bitterly. "It's bad enough getting meals ready at all hours of the day and night. And now it will be extra work to fix baby food and heat milk and wash dirty bottles until I'm blue in the face!"

The two fell silent as they saw Nancy and Bess. However, when the girls laughed, the servants decided that they were friendly and would not carry tales to the Blairs.

Despite her complaint, the cook willingly went to the refrigerator for milk when Nancy requested it.

"I don't begrudge the poor little tikes their food," she said in a softened mood. "It's the Blairs that give me a pain! They make out they're so crazy about kids, but if they find out the twins can't be trained for the stage, you can bet they'll get rid of 'em quick enough."

"Mrs. Blair carries on something awful when she's at a party," Colleen added. "The next day she don't get up until noon. She quarrels with her husband most of the time, too. Some atmosphere to bring up a pair of kids in, if you ask me!"

The girls did not care to listen to gossip, so as soon as the milk was ready they carried it back to the nursery. Colleen watched them feed the babies, and then helped to undress the twins and put them to sleep. The girls were accordingly relieved to learn that she was not entirely ignorant of the care of children.

Nancy observed that it was growing dark outside. Also, her wrist watch reminded her that Hannah would be coming along at any moment. Preferring to meet the housekeeper without being seen by the Blairs or their guests, Nancy quietly descended the back stairs and left the mansion by way of a side door.

Rounding a wing of the house she halted abruptly. A man was seated on a stone bench directly in her path. She could not reach the front drive without going by him.

Then something about his appearance held Nancy's attention. She could not see his face distinctly in the darkness, but she thought he resembled Rodney, the chauffeur. It was his position which she noted particularly. He leaned over dejectedly, and poked with his shoe absently at the cobblestones. She heard him sigh deeply.

"Poor man!" she thought sympathetically.

She was tempted to step forward and speak to him. Before she could act, however, he wearily arose and slowly walked away.

The sound of an automobile turning into the drive aroused Nancy from her momentary reverie. Hurrying forward, she was relieved to see that the approaching vehicle was a taxi. Hannah Gruen stepped from the cab, greeting her young mistress somewhat reproachfully.

"Of all the wild chases this is the worst! I declare, Nancy, I don't know what you'll think of next!"

"You're a dear to go to so much trouble for me," Nancy praised, turning to ask the taxi driver to wait. "Did you bring the things, Hannah?"

Hannah thrust a small bundle into the girl's arms.

"Here it is. But if you're aiming to bring those babies home with you, I may have something to say about it."

"Why, Hannah, don't you like babies?" Nancy teased.

"I like them all right, but I don't enjoy turning myself into a nursemaid! Your father won't be able to do a bit of work with two crying babies in the house."

Nancy laughed and squeezed the housekeeper's plump arm.

"Now don't you worry, Hannah. I'm not planning to bring the twins home with me."

"Then what do you want with these doll clothes? If I've made this trip out here for nothing——"

"You haven't," Nancy soothed her. "I can't explain anything now, but I think I've stumbled upon something important."

"You mean another mystery?" Hannah asked in awe.

"Perhaps."

"You didn't tell enough over the phone even to let me catch on," the housekeeper said in the tone of a fellow conspirator. "I'm glad to help you all I can, Nancy, though goodness knows my hands are more useful than my mind!"

"You've been a great help to me tonight," Nancy praised her. "You must hurry away before someone sees you."

She urged the good lady into the cab, and saw her safely on her way back to River Heights.

"And now for my little scheme!" Nancy said to herself. "I hope things work out all right."

Seating herself on the stone bench, she hastily ripped open the bundle. Hannah had obeyed orders implicitly, and had brought two white doll dresses. Nancy decided that they would pass for the garments which Jay and Janet had worn at one time, providing they were not examined too minutely.

She did not find the locket at once. But as she shook one of the dresses, there dropped to the ground the piece of jewelry she had worn a few years before. Nancy studied the heart-shaped gold trinket with great perplexity.

"I must find some way to break it in half," she reflected. "Otherwise, the Blairs will see at first glance that it isn't the one they have."

She tried bending back the hinge, but the locket was well made and refused to break.

"If I only had something hard to pound it against!"

She noticed a sharp stone almost at her feet and snatched it up. One firm blow, and the hinge parted.

Nancy now held two golden hearts in her hand. Each half closely resembled the broken locket in the bundle upstairs.

"Few persons would ever notice the difference," she chortled inwardly.

At that moment, when success seemed within her grasp, her keen ears detected the sound of footsteps. Nervously she glanced about, but could see no one in the dark.

"Who are you?" a woman's voice demanded sharply from directly behind her. "What are you doing?"

CHAPTER V

A DARING SCHEME

INVOLUNTARILY Nancy sprang to her feet, hiding the doll garments and the broken halves of the locket behind her back. She was grateful that darkness covered her movements, which she felt had been awkward.

Mrs. Dunbar emerged from the shadows.

"Why, it's you, Miss Drew!" she exclaimed.

"Yes," Nancy stammered. "I—I was just out for a little air."

"Don't blame you a bit," the actress said thickly. "Out for air myself. Stupid party. Didn't mean to speak so sharply. Just wanted to know what you were doing."

"Oh, just looking at something. I must hurry back to the nursery now."

She moved away swiftly before the actress could question her further, or see what it was that she was holding behind her back. Without being detected, she slipped into the house and upstairs.

Bess was alone in the nursery with the sleeping twins.

"Oh, did you get the things?" she cried,

spying the bundle. "I thought I heard a car drive up."

"I hope the Blairs didn't hear it."

"I doubt it. They were playing too loudly on the piano at the time for them to pay attention to anything outside."

"We must get away from here without further delay, Bess. I hope Colleen won't be back for at least a minute or two."

"I don't believe she will. She's expecting a young man to call and went downstairs to wait for him."

"Good! It will take me only a second to change these bundles."

Deftly she substituted the doll clothes for the baby garments, and thrust into her purse the broken locket which had come with the twins.

"I'm taking no chances on losing that bit of jewelry," she told Bess. "I have a hunch it may be of use some day in proving the parentage of these poor babies."

The girls were momentarily undecided as to how to carry away the baby clothes, for they dared not leave the house with a bundle which would excite suspicion. Nancy solved the problem by suggesting that they conceal the tiny garments in their bérets. After hiding the dresses beneath their headgear, the girls looked at themselves critically in the mirror.

"We'll get by, all right, if we can manage

to keep our bérets on," Nancy decided. She bent down to kiss the sleeping babies good-bye.

"I dislike leaving them here, Bess."

"So do I. I wish they had a real mother."

"If we can find her, they shall be restored to her!" Nancy announced. "I'll find some way to force Mrs. Blair to give up the children."

Feeling somewhat self-conscious, the girls descended to the living room.

"Why, you have your coats on!" Johnny Blair cried in protest. "You're not going yet! The party's just starting."

"Really, we *must* go," Nancy interrupted him impatiently.

"At least, let us pay you for your trouble," Johnny Blair insisted.

"No, thank you. Bess and I were glad to do what we could for the twins. They are going to need a great deal of mothering."

That subtle suggestion fell upon deaf ears, but it recalled something to Kitty Blair's befogged mind.

"Oh, I'll make a wonderful mother," she boasted. "That reminds me—we must have the ceremony."

"What ceremony?" her husband demanded.

"To celebrate my motherhood. We must get rid of the ghost of that other mother once and for all. Burn up all the evidence!"

Nancy and Bess exchanged anxious glances.

"Sure," Johnny Blair seconded his wife, "let's burn the evidence. Where is it?"

"Upstairs. Colleen left the bundle in the nursery. Get it, Johnny, like a good boy."

Again the girls moved to depart, but the protests of the guests made it impossible for them to do so. Kitty tried to induce them to take off their coats and bérets, but they were adamant on this point.

Johnny returned presently with the bundle which Nancy and Bess had substituted for the real baby clothes and locket. He was in jubilant spirits.

"The fire is burning low," Kitty complained. "We must have a good blaze. Send for Rodney to bring in some more logs."

One of the guests went out to find the chauffeur. When he did not come at once, Kitty grew impatient.

The idea of a grand "motherhood" ceremony had been merely a notion and passed away as suddenly as it had come.

"Oh, what's the difference?" she cried. "Someone toss the bundle into the flames and we'll be done with it."

As no one made a move to do so, she carelessly caught up the parcel and flung it into the embers.

Fascinated, everyone watched. The paper became scorched, then burst into flames. Tiny blue and red tongues darted up about the flimsy white garments.   The broken locket lay exposed.

Nancy and Bess were immeasurably happy that they had saved the real bundle and locket. Nevertheless, it was an uncomfortable moment for them.   They feared that Kitty Blair might notice the substitution.

"The twins are really mine now!" the actress cried.   "If the parents should ever turn up, there wouldn't be a scrap of evidence to prove their right to the babies!"

At that moment Rodney appeared in the doorway with fresh logs, which Mrs. Blair bade him throw on the fire.   The chauffeur moved forward to obey.   His gaze traveled to the hearth and the tiny white garments which were ablaze.

Suddenly the logs slipped out of his arms to the floor.   A strangled cry of anguish escaped from his lips and his face changed to an ashen hue.   Then he pitched forward in a faint.

Kitty Blair emitted a piercing scream and slumped upon the sofa.   She recovered herself quickly, when no one paid the slightest heed to her cries.

The guests were momentarily too stunned by the accident to make a helpful move.   It was Nancy alone who had sufficient presence of mind to pull the unconscious man away from the hearth before he was seriously burned.

"Oh, oh, he's dead!" Mrs. Dunbar moaned,

wringing her hands. "What shall we do? What shall we do?"

"He's only fainted, I think," Nancy said calmly. "Help me turn him over."

Bess, recovering from her fright, darted forward to aid her chum. By this time Phil Dunbar and Johnny Blair had gained control of themselves, and they, too, offered assistance.

Carefully the man was lifted and turned over. Then a little gasp of astonishment burst from the lips of those who had gathered about him. They stared at Rodney's forehead in fascinated horror. Burned into the skin just above the right eye was the distinct imprint of a heart!

"See!" Kitty cried in terror. "A red heart! It's an evil omen!"

The guests were frightened and half stupefied.

"It's a warning to you because you burned the baby clothes, Kitty," Boots Dunbar murmured in awe. "I'm glad *I* didn't throw the bundle into the fire."

"Maybe we shouldn't have adopted the twins," Johnny said nervously. "They may bring us bad luck."

Nancy made a swift observation of her own. When Rodney had pitched face downward into the embers, his forehead had come in direct contact with the hot metal of the broken heart-shaped locket. Naturally, it had left its mark.

Although no one wanted to touch the man, Phil and Johnny reluctantly lifted him from the floor. Bess ran to the kitchen for water. Before she returned with it, the chauffeur had regained consciousness.

Everyone was greatly relieved, although the telltale imprint of the heart continued to hold them spellbound. Had it not been for Nancy and Bess, little would have been done for the comfort of the unfortunate chauffeur. His eyes fluttered open and he stared vacantly about the room.

"What happened?" he gasped.

"You fainted," Nancy told him gently, pressing a glass of water to his lips. "Here, drink this and you'll feel better."

The man did as he was bidden. Wearily he dropped his head back against the pillows Bess thrust behind him.

"I remember now," he said slowly. "I came into the room and saw—" His voice trailed off. Then he continued:

"I was gassed in the World War. Haven't been strong since. When the air gets close in a room, I don't seem to be able to breathe."

"Don't try to talk," Nancy soothed. "Just lie back and rest. I'll bandage your head," she added, not wanting the man to see the burn, for she feared that the sight of the red heart might unnerve him.

She hardly knew what to make of Rodney's

explanation. His gaunt appearance bore out his words; no doubt he had been gassed in the war. But certainly the burning baby garments had been the cause of his faint. Why should the sight have distressed him so greatly?

Nancy found a medicine cabinet in a bathroom. With Bess's assistance she made a neat bandage about Rodney's head. She was relieved to see the color returning to his face. With the windows open he breathed normally again.

Nancy could not fail to notice that his eyes frequently roved toward the fireplace. Yet whenever they did so, an expression of pain would cross his face.

"I must find a way of drawing him out later," she thought. "He may know something about the twins."

The girls had done all they possibly could for the chauffeur. Cautioning the Blairs to keep him quiet for a day at least, they prepared to leave the place.

"Miss Drew, you are simply marvelous!" Mrs. Blair gushed gratefully. "I don't know what we'd have done——"

The sentence was never finished.

From upstairs there came a loud thud, followed by the crash of glassware. Then a girl's piercing scream rent the air!

CHAPTER VI

A NIGHT OF MISHAPS

No ONE moved for the space of an instant.
Then Nancy and her chum darted up the stairway, while the Blairs and their guests stood
staring as though paralyzed with fear. The
girls judged from the sound that the crash had
come from the general direction of the nursery.

"Oh, I wonder if anything has happened to
the babies!" Bess exclaimed anxiously.

One glimpse into the babies' room assured
them that nothing was amiss there. The twins
were sleeping peacefully in their cribs.

"Then it must have come from the servants'
quarters," Nancy decided.

They rushed to the back stairs which led
down to the kitchen. On a landing lay Colleen
in a heap, moaning. All about her were strewn
jagged fragments of nursing bottles.

"Are you hurt?" Nancy cried, hurrying
down to assist her.

She lifted the sobbing Colleen to her feet.

"It's my arm! I've cut it!"

The Blairs and their guests were hastening
down the stairway. Nancy led the girl to the

44

kitchen, there to examine the cut under a light.

"What happened?" she questioned.

"I was carrying the empty bottles from the nursery when I caught my shoe in a torn place in the stair carpet." The weeping Colleen cast Mrs. Blair a reproachful glance to remind the actress that she had promised to have the hole repaired. "Down I went, the bottles on top of me. I might have been killed!"

"But you weren't," Nancy said cheerfully, for she saw that the girl was more frightened than hurt.

"You should watch where you're going!" Mrs. Blair told her tartly.

"Let me see your arm," Nancy suggested.

Colleen obligingly held out the injured member. There was only a slight flesh wound, but Nancy stared at it in fascinated amazement. By some strange coincidence the wound had taken the intricate shape of a heart. Anyone with a vivid imagination could easily fancy that the mark had been caused by some evil influence.

"Another heart!" Kitty Blair cried, staring blankly. "Oh! Oh!"

She toppled over in a faint and would have fallen to the floor, had not her husband caught her in his arms.

For several minutes everything was in confusion, Nancy herself scarcely knowing which way to turn. Colleen began to weep again;

Mrs. Dunbar grew hysterical; the guests dashed about the kitchen getting in one another's way, and accomplishing nothing.

Johnny revived his wife by dashing a glass of cold water into her face. She opened her eyes, sputtering angrily.

"You've ruined my best gown, you stupid man!" she berated. Then her eye fell upon Colleen and she became greatly excited again, calling out, "Take her away! Take her away!"

Nancy and Bess led Colleen to the nursery, where they washed and bandaged the cut.

"What did Mrs. Blair mean when she cried 'another heart'?" the girl demanded.

"Oh, it was just a superstitious idea of hers," Nancy replied carelessly. "Don't worry about it."

"Something about the babies, I'll bet!" the maid guessed shrewdly. "You know, ever since I came here strange things have been happening!"

"Nonsense!" Nancy laughed.

"It isn't nonsense. The cook predicted that bad luck would follow the children into the house, and I believe she's right!"

Nothing the girls said altered Colleen's belief that the twins had a "sign" upon them.

"Whatever you do, don't suggest such a silly idea to Mrs. Blair," Nancy warned her as she left the maid.

Returning to the living room, the girls found that Kitty Blair had recovered her composure somewhat. Nevertheless, she still appeared shaken up and frightened.

"I almost wish now that I hadn't burned the baby clothes," she told Nancy. "If anything should happen to ruin my career, I'd know it was the result of that one act."

The hour had grown late. Nancy and Bess were tired, while the latter was particularly eager to return home lest her parents worry. Hastily they bade good-bye to the guests, promising to return again some day.

"I intend to keep that promise, too," Nancy informed her chum as they hurried to the waiting automobile. "Not because I find the Blairs such splendid company, however."

"Aren't they disgusting! So very shallow-minded and superstitious."

"Yes. If all theatrical people were of their caliber, I'd never care to go to another show. But they're certainly not like most actors."

The girls entered the car. As soon as they were a safe distance from the estate, they removed the baby garments from their bérets.

"Such an evening!" Bess exclaimed. "I'm all tired out."

"So am I. Even so, we have accomplished our purpose. We have the bundle we went after."

"And we know a great deal about the Blairs

and their frivolous friends," Bess added. "I'm getting very interested in the case, Nancy."

"Glad you came along?"

"Am I? You'll keep me posted on any developments that may arise, won't you?"

"Yes, indeed," Nancy promised.

"I am certain you'll find the parents of the twins," her chum maintained firmly. "You can do anything you make up your mind to do."

Nancy laughed.

"I'm not so certain of that."

"Look at the complicated mysteries you've cleared up in the past. And you have splendid evidence to work on in this case."

"The locket may be a clue," Nancy admitted.

"And it seems to me you have uncovered another clue in Rodney," Bess pointed out eagerly. "Did you notice how he kept looking at the burning baby clothes in the fireplace?"

"Yes, I noticed that especially."

"It struck me that there was a connection of some kind between him and the twins," Bess went on. "Though he may have been gassed in the war, it's my opinion he fainted when he saw that bundle burning, and not from the effects of his overseas experience."

"He certainly was affected by the sight. Still, we mustn't jump hastily at conclusions. Circumstantial evidence isn't always correct evidence, you know."

"Just the same, I think Rodney knows something about the twins," Bess maintained. "Maybe he's their father!"

"Now that is an idea!" Nancy laughed. "Did you notice any resemblance?"

"Oh, stop teasing, Nancy Drew! Of course I didn't. I know my ideas are absurd."

"They're not!" Nancy said quickly. "To tell you the truth, I thought the very same thing."

"You did!"

"Yes, but I'm not allowing myself to believe a thing without the necessary proof. We must make haste slowly."

"Of course. If Mrs. Blair suspected that we were intending to interfere in her affairs, she'd make serious trouble."

"That's the way I figure it. We must keep this thing under our hats until we have definite proof as to the babies' parentage."

"Under our bérets, you mean," Bess chuckled. "We started out that way, at least!"

Nancy drove rapidly and soon reached River Heights. She dropped Bess off at the Marvin home, again cautioning her to the strictest secrecy.

A light was burning in Carson Drew's study when she finally reached home. She found her father nervously pacing the floor.

"I've been worrying about you," he confessed. "Hannah had a weird tale to report when she returned from Jolly Folly."

"I should think she must have," Nancy laughed.

Just then she caught a glimpse of the housekeeper at the door and knew that the good woman was fairly beside herself with anxiety, fearing that her young mistress had brought the twins home.

"You may as well come in, Hannah," Nancy invited.

Somewhat sheepishly, the housekeeper entered. She continued to eye the girl dubiously, and cast a quick glance about the study.

"You needn't worry," Nancy told her with an amused smile. "I left the babies with Mrs. Blair."

"Oh, I was afraid you might do something impulsive," Hannah returned in evident relief. "It isn't that I don't like babies, only——"

"You like them at a distance," Nancy teased. "I did feel tempted to bring the darlings home with me, but I knew that would never do."

After the housekeeper had left the study, Nancy turned to her father, showing him the locket and the children's garments.

"This is what my evening netted me, Dad. What do you think of my haul?"

Curiously Mr. Drew examined the articles. He did not look as impressed as Nancy had expected he would.

"You did well to obtain these things," he said briskly. "However, I'm afraid you must have more substantial evidence than this to get anywhere in this case."

"Then you think the clothes won't be of any help?"

"The garments haven't a mark or initial of any kind on them."

"I thought the broken locket might be of real significance in solving this mystery."

"Perhaps."

Carson Drew turned the curious trinket over in his hand, examining it closely under the light. It was made of gold, and was an exquisite piece of craftsmanship, finely wrought. Yet there was no initial, inscription, or picture of any kind upon it.

"You haven't much to start on, Nancy."

"I realize that. But I have a feeling that if I just keep on plugging away, something may turn up."

"Then I don't want to discourage you. After all, success is ninety per cent perspiration and only ten per cent inspiration!"

"I'll keep these articles, anyway," Nancy decided, wrapping the clothing into a neat bundle. "If the twins' mother should appear some day, I can at least give these to her. Then she'll have a few things to remember her babies by."

"I tried to do a little detective work myself after you left," Carson Drew said abruptly as his daughter turned to leave.

"You did? What did you learn?"

"Nothing. I don't seem to have your luck, Nancy. It occurred to me to try to trace that telegram which was signed 'Broken Heart.' But that was impossible."

"Perhaps the woman will try to get in touch with us personally a little later," Nancy commented hopefully.

"She may, though I doubt it. The afternoon paper had a story about the adoption. When the mother sees it, she'll know that it is too late for her to do anything."

The attorney spread the paper out upon his desk for Nancy to read. On a half-page layout were the pictures of the twins, together with flattering poses of their new parents, Kitty and Johnny Blair.

"Why, this copy must have been prepared ahead of time," she remarked, frowning.

"The Blairs' publicity agent isn't overlooking anything," her father returned dryly.

"Father, you said something a minute ago that I didn't exactly agree with," Nancy remarked after a pause. "You stated that if the mother of the twins were to see this paper, she would know it was too late for her to do anything. Did you mean that?"

Mr. Drew hesitated before answering.

"The adoption papers are signed, Nancy. Even if you should be successful in tracing the mother of the babies, I'm not convinced that matters could be adjusted."

"But surely any court would award a mother her own children!"

"That depends upon several factors, Nancy. Usually a court does not look with favor upon a woman who abandons her offspring."

"There isn't any real proof that she did. As I understand it—though my information is scant—the babies were found during a storm. Perhaps they were accidentally separated from their parents."

"That might have been the case."

"I mean to go to the Selkirk Home one of these days and learn all the details," Nancy continued.

"I see that you don't intend to give up the search," Mr. Drew smiled.

"Indeed not. I know it's foolish of me, but I keep thinking of those helpless twins and what a miserable life they'll have if Kitty Blair rears them."

"My little girl is very tender-hearted," the attorney said, drawing her down upon the arm of the easy chair. "I'm glad you are that way, though."

Nancy gave him a kiss, and then rumpled his hair.

"You're a peach, Father," she laughed. "You let me do anything I like and never make fun of my wild ideas."

Before Mr. Drew could respond, the doorbell rang. Nancy sprang to her feet, thrusting the broken locket and the bundle of baby clothes into a convenient desk drawer.

"Sit still, Father. I'll answer. It's probably one of the girls."

As she opened the door, great was her surprise to see standing before her the Reverend Doctor Paul Stafford. He was a kindly, middle-aged man, pastor of a church in the opposite end of the city from the Drew home. This was the first time he had ever called, although Nancy knew him well by sight.

"Why, good evening, Doctor Stafford," she greeted him. "Won't you come in?"

"Yes, I must see your father if he is at home. I am sorry to trouble him at this late hour, but what I have to tell him is important."

"Father is in his study."

Nancy observed that the minister appeared somewhat agitated as she conducted him to Mr. Drew. She turned to leave, but before she could reach the door he broached the subject of his mission.

"Mr. Drew, I've come to talk about a rather odd matter," he began slowly. "This afternoon a woman came to my parsonage—a total stranger. She begged me to carry a message to you."

At these words Nancy became supremely alert. Her sense of intuition told her that the minister's visitor had some connection with the twins.

CHAPTER VII

A STRANGE CALLER

"Do you mind if my daughter hears what you have to say?" Carson Drew inquired, for out of the corner of his eye he had noted Nancy's apparent interest.

"Not at all," the minister returned. "In fact, she may be able to help me. I have heard of her admirable record in solving mysteries."

"What is this message you were requested to deliver to me?" Mr. Drew queried.

The pastor looked a trifle embarrassed.

"No doubt it will sound odd. As I said before, a strange woman, highly strung and emotional, called at my home today. I was preparing my weekly sermon at the time. At first she talked about things in general, but I suspected all the while that she was in trouble.

"In due course of time she spoke out, asking me to deliver a message to you, Mr. Drew. I suggested that she call at your office, but for some reason she seemed unwilling to do so."

"Peculiar, to say the least," the attorney commented. "But you haven't told me her secret."

55

"I'm coming to it. She said, 'You must plead with Mr. Drew not to permit the twin babies to be adopted by the Blairs.' Before I could question her further, she had left. I'm sure it sounds a trifle nonsensical, but my conscience would not allow me to rest had I failed to inform you. For some reason or other, the tragic expression on the woman's face remains in my memory, and I cannot forget it."

Nancy and her father exchanged significant glances. The message was perfectly clear to both of them. Doubtless the mysterious visitor was the woman who had signed herself "Broken Heart" in the telegram to Mr. Drew. For some unknown reason, perhaps because she feared legal entanglements, she had hesitated to call upon the attorney personally.

"I'm sorry to have taken your time at such a late hour," the pastor continued apologetically. "I rather suspect that the poor woman was suffering from some sort of an obsession."

"I am inclined to believe that her message is perfectly rational," Mr. Drew returned. "However, it is too late for me to do anything. The twins of whom she spoke have been adopted already."

Briefly, then, he told the Reverend Doctor Stafford a few of the circumstances incident to the adoption case. The minister was plainly impressed.

"The poor woman may have been the mother

of the babies," he remarked sadly. "I regret now that I did not detain her."

Nancy had been listening intently to the conversation. She could not refrain from asking a few questions.

"Can you describe the person who came to your house, Doctor Stafford?"

The minister looked perplexed.

"I must confess I am somewhat inattentive to details. She had a pleasing face, though very sad in expression. She was of average height, I should judge, but extremely thin. Her dark hair was flecked with gray."

"Then she was middle-aged?"

"No. I shouldn't say that. She may have been thirty or thirty-five, but trouble rather than years has no doubt aged her."

"Did you notice anything outstanding about her?" remarked Nancy.

"I can't say that I did, unless it was her voice, which was one of the most musical I have ever heard. At one time she might have been a singer."

"Did you observe how she was dressed?" Nancy probed.

"Her clothes were neat, but plain. She wore a gray suit, I believe, and a black felt hat with a red quill on it. During the entire conversation I had the strangest feeling—it was as if I had seen her at some time."

"And yet you never had?" Mr. Drew asked.

"I was confident that I had never set eyes upon her before. My wife could not place her, either."

"I wish there was some way in which to trace her," Nancy said thoughtfully. "Has she left River Heights yet?"

"It is my opinion that she came here from another city. In fact, she appeared at my home shortly after the arrival of the afternoon train. I recall, too, that she frequently consulted her watch. I infer that she boarded a later train."

"We appreciate your coming here tonight," said Mr. Drew gratefully. "Rest assured that if anything can be done to aid this unfortunate woman, my daughter and I shall make every effort to straighten out her troubles."

"I am very glad I came to see you, Mr. Drew. As I said before, the woman's face haunts me. Then, too, I have always had a deep interest in twins."

"You have?" Nancy encouraged eagerly. "Why is that?"

The minister, thus invited to prolong his stay, settled back in his chair, adjusted his gold spectacles, and launched into a story to which Mr. Drew and his daughter listened with keen interest.

"Years ago, when I was a young man and had just graduated from the seminary and had been ordained, I was new to my parish and highly nervous. The thought of conducting the first baptismal service flustered me." Doctor Stafford chuckled at the memory.

"How long ago was that?" Nancy interposed.

"Let me see—it must have been all of thirty years."

The churchman paused.

"Do go on!" Nancy urged.

"As I was saying, the thought of my first baptismal service made me quite nervous. I hoped that everything would go off well. Imagine my confusion when a woman came up to the altar with twins in her arms!"

"What were the names of the twins?" Nancy asked as he paused.

"The names? Now, let me see. Ruth was the baby girl's name. Oh, yes, I baptized them, Ruth and Rodney. Rather pretty names, too, I thought."

"Rodney?" Nancy gasped. "Did you say Rodney?"

"Yes, I am sure that was it." The minister stared curiously at her, wondering why she was so interested.

Mr. Drew likewise threw a quick glance at his daughter. He knew her well enough to realize that she had stumbled upon some clue which was not apparent to him.

Actually, Nancy had no clue. But when the minister mentioned the name Rodney it was only natural that her thoughts should revert to the Blairs' chauffeur. She knew nothing of his family or his past, yet his almost uncanny interest in the bundle of baby garments which had belonged to the twins had stamped him indelibly upon her memory.

"What was the last name of the babies whom you baptized?" she questioned eagerly.

"Let me think. I should recall, but it seems to have slipped my mind. Slight wonder after all these years."

"Did you keep a record of the names?" Nancy inquired hopefully.

"Why yes, I have it at home. If you really would like to know what they are, I think I can perhaps find them for you."

"I'd appreciate it very much," Nancy assured him. "I know my request seems strange. I don't mind telling you that I think the twins whom you baptized might have some connection with the present case."

The pastor regarded her incredulously. Even Mr. Drew looked a trifle doubtful. Doctor Stafford arose to leave.

"If I find the records, I will bring them to you at once," he promised Nancy as she conducted him to the door. "And I hope something can be done about those unfortunate children adopted by the Blairs."

The Drew girl and her father returned to the study after the pastor had left.

"Drawing rather hasty conclusions, aren't

you?'' Mr. Drew remarked to his daughter as they faced each other. ''For years I've prided myself upon being a lawyer of average intelligence, yet I'm frank to admit I can see not the slightest connection between the twins Ruth and Rodney and the Blairs' adopted babies.''

Nancy laughed.

''Well, Father, maybe you're right and I'm wrong, but I was very much interested in what the minister said.''

''Just what were you driving at?''

''I don't exactly know myself—yet! The Blairs have a chauffeur named Rodney, a sad, lean sort of individual who was gassed in the World War.''

''There must be hundreds of Rodneys in the state, Nancy!''

''I know the name isn't of much help. But the thing that struck me as strange was the way this chauffeur fainted when he saw the bundle of baby clothes burning.''

''Perhaps he fainted from other causes. You say he was gassed in the war.''

''He doesn't look well,'' Nancy admitted.

''Nevertheless, I'm convinced that he was unnerved by the sight of that package.''

''You surely don't mean to imply that he is the father of the twins!''

''I'm not implying anything—I'm only wondering.''

Carson Drew could not restrain a smile.

"Your little 'wonderer' is taking you on a wild flight this time, I think, Nancy. Mind, I'm not saying you aren't right."

"But you're thinking it," she accused him. "Oh, well, I know the conjecture is far fetched. For that matter, I'm not certain I believe it myself."

"It may not be a bad idea to trace down the names of those twins, Ruth and Rodney," the attorney went on, observing that his words had discouraged Nancy. "Queer information occasionally comes out from unexpected sources. By the way, what is this chauffeur's last name?"

Nancy was forced to admit that she did not know.

"I can find out easily enough, though. So many exciting things were going on while I was at the Blair place that I didn't have time to ask his name."

"You did have a stimulating evening. You always seem to be able to stir up excitement wherever you go."

"I didn't do any stirring tonight," Nancy countered. "I was busy most of the time quieting down things. If ever a place was a bedlam, Jolly Folly was it!"

"I didn't think you'd save that bundle of garments when you went out there," Mr. Drew remarked teasingly. "Are you sure you didn't bring back any silverware or furniture?"

"I wouldn't have any of their gaudy things if they'd give them to me! Do you think it was wrong to exchange the baby clothes and the locket?"

"Of course not. It was all done in a worthy cause."

"That's what I thought. If I hadn't preserved them, the last scrap of evidence linking Jay and Janet to the past would have been destroyed."

Mr. Drew nodded.

"Speaking of evidence, I noticed you received a bit from Reverend Stafford. Stole the show right away from your old dad."

"I didn't mean to do that, only when you pause so long between questions, I can't keep quiet. I was determined to know what that woman who called upon him looked like."

"His description may be of value to you. Nancy, I want to say I was impressed with the story. I'm inclined to believe that the woman who sent us that telegram and the one who called upon Doctor Stafford are one and the same person."

"I'm sure of it myself."

Mr. Drew arose to turn out the study light, for it was way past his usual bedtime.

"I've had a hard day, Nancy. I think I'll get some sleep."

"Yes, Father, I can see you are very tired. I'll be along in a few minutes. Goodnight."

For fully an hour after Mr. Drew had retired, Nancy sat in the living room mulling over the information she had gleaned. She inferred from her parent's attitude that he doubted her ability to straighten out the tangled past of little Jay and Janet.

"I guess I was born to involve myself in hopeless problems," she thought as she climbed the stairs to her bedroom. "But I've been puzzled before, and I may find a way out of this."

So weary was Nancy from her day's adventure that she fell asleep almost the instant her head touched the pillow. Her dreams were troubled. She visualized a court room scene in which a weeping mother stood pleading for her babies. She saw the leering, triumphant faces of the Blairs as the judge awarded them custody of the children.

"That dream was almost too realistic," Nancy told her father the next morning at breakfast. "I hope it isn't a premonition."

Although she was determined to do all she could to find the parents of the twins, Nancy's enthusiasm for the project did not run at the same fever heat as it had on the previous day. The obstacles to be surmounted looked larger than ever.

While she was finishing her breakfast, she was called to the telephone by Hannah.

"It's from out in the country, I think," the

housekeeper said. "The words didn't come in well over the line."

Nancy took down the receiver. At first she did not recognize the voice.

"This is Colleen Walsh at the Jolly Folly estate!"

Nancy was instantly alert.

"Try to talk slower," she requested. "I can't understand you very well."

"I'm here all by myself, save for the servants," Colleen told her shrilly. "I'm having an awful time with the babies."

"They aren't ill?" Nancy demanded anxiously.

"No, the twins are all right, only they cry a lot, but I can't hold them. It's my arm. It hurts me all the time."

There was a slight hesitation; then the nursemaid suggested timidly:

"I thought perhaps you or your friend would be willing to come out and help me."

Nancy had anticipated this request. It was somewhat unfair of the girl to expect Bess or herself to do such work, but if Colleen really needed aid she would not refuse her. Then, too, a day spent at Jolly Folly might add to Nancy's store of information concerning the Blairs and their chauffeur, Rodney.

"I'll see if I can get in touch with Bess," Nancy promised. "I feel confident she'll come. We'll drive out as quickly as we can."

CHAPTER VIII

A Mysterious Lady

Nancy telephoned Bess Marvin without delay, and was delighted to find her chum willing to make the trip to Jolly Folly.

"I'll be ready in a little while if you'll stop for me," she agreed. "I have some work to finish, but it won't take me long."

Promptly at ten-thirty Nancy drove up to the Marvin residence, where Bess awaited her on the veranda. True to her agreement to keep her friend informed regarding any developments concerning the adoption, Nancy at once reported Doctor Stafford's visit of the previous night.

"Clues just seem to fall into your hands," Bess marveled.

"I hope a few fall my way today, but I don't expect such good luck."

As they were driving by a department store Nancy impulsively suggested that they purchase some toys for the twins.

"Fine!" Bess approved, "only I didn't bring much money with me."

"I have enough for both of us."

Parking room was at a premium on the busy main street. Nancy finally found a small space, and to the admiration of her chum maneuvered her car into it.

"You could turn on a dime, Nancy," laughed Bess.

The store was not crowded. The girls were waited upon in no time, but it was not easy for them to make their selections. Finally, after much deliberation, Nancy chose a cleverly stuffed dog which was nearly as large as little Jay himself, while Bess purchased a bright red ball for Janet.

The parcels were wrapped up, and a few minutes later the girls were once more on their way. They had covered little more than half the distance when Nancy's keen eyes sighted a familiar car far down the road.

"Isn't that the Blairs' automobile, Bess?"

"Why, I believe it is!"

"Colleen told me they would be away for the day."

By this time the machine was drawing closer and closer. Nancy slowed down, ready to stop if the Blairs should hail her.

The approaching car was moving at a moderate rate of speed. As it passed the girls, neither Mr. and Mrs. Blair nor Rodney, who was at the wheel, chanced to look in their direction.

"The car was loaded down with golf clubs,"

Bess observed. "Out for a day at the country club, I suppose."

"Kitty probably is celebrating her motherhood!" Nancy returned with a short laugh. "She adopted the twins only yesterday, yet she can't stay home and look after them for even a day!"

"Imagine what it will be like when she's had the babies for a month or so and the novelty has worn off! I think they should be taken from her!"

"The little things deserve a real mother," Nancy agreed feelingly. "If we can't find their parents, I wish someone could have them who would really love them."

"I'd like to have them myself," Bess said wistfully. "I suggested the idea to Mother last night and she nearly fainted."

"Hannah is like that, too. She doesn't want any babies, dogs, cats, or anything lively about the place."

"Wouldn't it be a strange situation if the chauffeur Rodney should turn out to be the twins' father?" Bess speculated. "It would be hard for him in that case to live in the same household, yet be unable to claim them as his own children."

"And see them neglected," Nancy added.

"We must watch him closely. I'm sorry he'll be away for the day."

"So am I. I was looking forward to a long

talk with him. I wonder at the Blairs expecting him to drive their car today when he should be in bed.''

''I imagine they work all their servants too hard. All save Colleen—'' she added, with a laugh. ''I doubt if anyone will ever get the best of the nursemaid that way.''

Nancy had reached Jolly Folly and turned the car into the winding driveway. A maid conducted the girls without delay to the nursery. Somewhat to their surprise, they found Colleen at work.

She was attempting to bathe the babies. In the struggle, the twins appeared to have gained the mastery. Jay was splashing gleefully about in the tub, covering the floor and the distraught maid with water. Janet would emit frightened squeals of terror whenever a drop of water would touch her.

''Oh, I'm so glad you've come!'' Colleen murmured, sinking down into the nearest chair and abandoning the babies to their fate. ''My arm is paining me so, and this eternal yelling and crying is driving me wild!''

''I don't believe you have bathed many babies,'' Bess declared, springing forward to prevent Jay from eating the soap. ''Why didn't you try washing them one at a time?''

''I never thought of that,'' Colleen admitted. ''I thought it would be easier to get it all over with at once.''

"It's the water that is all over," Nancy laughed. "You sit still and rest that arm. We'll take charge of the children."

Since the infants were shivering, the girls hastily gave them their baths. Bess was expert at dressing the twins.

Jay and Janet were delighted with their new toys, and invented a game of their own. Janet threw her ball across the room while Nancy ran to bring it back again. Jay, not to be excluded, tossed his dog into a far corner for Bess to retrieve. They repeated this procedure time and again.

"This threatens to become a marathon," Nancy laughed.

"It's like that all the time," Colleen told her wearily. "It's something every minute, and Mrs. Blair won't even carry up a milk bottle!"

Soon the twins were placed in their cribs. Nancy took advantage of the resultant quiet to ask a few questions.

"We met the Blairs and their chauffeur on the road this morning. By the way, Colleen, what is Rodney's last name?"

"Brown. He's a funny sort, too."

"In what way?" Nancy inquired quickly.

"Oh, I don't know—just peculiar. He sits around mooning over something half the time. Never goes out with girls. Doesn't say much to anybody."

"He was in the war, I was told."

"Yes, I guess he won some medals," the maid returned indifferently. "I know he was gassed. That was what was wrong with him when he fainted the other night. I heard him tell the cook so."

"The Blairs should have permitted him to rest today."

"And me, too! But you don't know them! They spend scads of money on themselves, yet check up on how much food the servants eat."

"And Rodney," Nancy murmured, for she did not wish the nursemaid to change the subject, "has he many friends?"

"Not him. I don't think he likes people."

"Where is his home?"

"I never asked. He was working for the Blairs before I came."

Colleen began to show signs of growing irritated at so many questions. She preferred to talk of her own young man friend and could not understand why Nancy should show the slightest interest in such a homely person as Rodney Brown.

"Tonight's supposed to be my night off," she remarked resentfully. "I'm dating Francis—that is, if Mrs. Blair gets back in time. If she's late I'll be furious."

"I don't believe we know Francis," Nancy said with a faint smile.

"He's swell!" Colleen's face grew radiant. "The most handsome man I ever met. Of course, he has red hair, but you get used to it."

"What is his last name?" Bess inquired curiously.

"Didn't I tell you? It's Clancy. Francis Clancy. He has a swell job, too! He's a detective."

"Does Mrs. Blair object to your dates?" Nancy asked with friendly interest.

"She objects to everything! But that's not the worst trouble. These twins complicate things so."

Colleen glanced almost resentfully at the cribs.

"You're paid to take care of the babies," Bess reminded her.

"Sure, but I didn't know it would be such a job when I said I'd do it. I was here as upstairs girl and personal maid to Mrs. Blair before she got the adoption idea."

The conversation was interrupted by the sound of a delivery truck driving up to the house. Colleen ran to the window.

"Why, they're unloading a baby carriage! Mrs. Blair must have ordered it."

Everyone hurried downstairs to examine the fine double perambulator.

"Let's take the twins for a ride!" Bess proposed. "It's a warm, sunny day and they need the air."

Accordingly the babies were given their noonday meal, and then dressed in fluffy, white suits. Colleen, however, took but slight interest in them, stating that while the girls were away she would lie down and rest.

"If the cook will give us a lunch to take with us, we won't need to come back for several hours," Nancy declared enthusiastically. "We can really explore the grounds."

The cook was very glad to pack a few sandwiches for the girls since it saved her the trouble of preparing a warm luncheon. They accordingly set off in high spirits, pushing the carriage ahead of them.

Nancy and Bess explored the flower garden, pausing to pick a bouquet of calendulas near a tiny, artificial pond containing goldfish. The twins laughed in high glee when a fat frog plumped from a lily-pad into the water.

The well-kept lawn of the Blair estate sloped gradually down to a winding river. There, under a spreading shade tree, the girls opened the lunch box.

"Don't look at me so greedily," Nancy laughed at Janet. "You have had your dinner."

After lunch the girls sat on the grass chatting while the babies fell asleep.

"Let's go wading in the cove," Bess proposed suddenly.

"Dare we leave the twins?"

"We'll be within sight of them. It's so hot today I'd like to cool off a little."

"All right. Let's set the carriage back from the bank where it cannot possibly be moved by the wind."

They found a safe place for the perambulator, out of the direct rays of the sun, yet within plain view of the cove. Nancy carefully set the brake on the wheel.

Then, feeling entirely care free, they raced toward the water with shouts of laughter. Nancy pulled off her shoes and stockings and placed them over the branches of a low-hanging tree. She splashed out into the shallow water and Bess soon followed.

"I haven't gone wading in years," Nancy laughed. "If Dad could see me now, he'd abandon all hope of rearing me to be a sedate young lady."

"Pooh! Who wants to grow up proper anyway?" Bess scoffed, splashing water. "I wish we could go swimming."

"So do I, but the water isn't deep enough and we have no suits. Oh, look, Bess!"

"A baby turtle!"

The girls became so absorbed in watching the awkward antics of the tiny reptile that for a time they quite forgot the carriage on the bank. When Nancy did look in that direction, she started.

A woman was standing beside the perambulator. As Nancy watched her, she quickly bent down and kissed the babies.

"Bess, who is that woman? It isn't Mrs. Blair, surely."

Bess was as startled as her chum.

"No, she's a stranger to me!"

With one accord the girls splashed through the water toward the bank. They did not propose to leave the twins alone with an unknown person, even though the individual might have the kindliest intentions in the world.

Hearing the sound of their approach the intruder glanced up, panic in her face. It was then that Nancy noticed the stranger's attire. She wore a gray suit and a close-fitting black felt hat. Her face was shaded, so the girls caught only a glimpse of it.

Again, to the amazement of Nancy and Bess, the woman stooped over and kissed the babies. Then she wheeled about and darted into the bushes.

"Wait!" Nancy called. "Please wait!"

There was no answer. The girls could hear the stranger running through the brush toward the main road.

"We must catch her if we can!" Nancy cried.

They did not stop long enough to slip on their shoes. Stones and pebbles gashed their feet as they ran, impeding their progress.

"We'll never catch her this way!" Bess exclaimed in anguish. "I'm cutting my feet till they're bleeding."

Nancy also realized that pursuit was use-

less. Reluctantly she halted. Instantly she
became alert again, holding up her hand for
Bess to listen. Suddenly the girls heard an
automobile start up the main road.

"She must have parked her car near here!"
Nancy cried. "And it sounds to me as if she's
heading toward River Heights!"

"Maybe you could catch her if you use the
roadster!"

"I'm going to try it, if you'll take the twins
to the house!"

"Of course."

Back they raced to the river where Nancy
put on her shoes and stockings in a twinkling.
Leaving Bess to wheel the babies to the house,
she darted off ahead. Then, dashing into her
automobile, she turned it into the main road.

Nancy was convinced that the stranger who
had kissed the babies was the same person who
had called at the home of the Reverend Doctor
Paul Stafford.

"I must catch her!" she thought, stepping
hard on the accelerator. "If I can induce her
to talk, I will feel certain she'll be able to clear
up the mystery of the twins' parentage!"

CHAPTER IX

A NEAR ACCIDENT

THE road ahead was clear. Pressing more firmly upon the gas pedal, Nancy made the figures roll rapidly across the dial of the speedometer. Far ahead, she caught sight of an automobile. A woman was at the wheel. There were no other passengers.

"I'm positive it's the same person!" she told herself tensely. "If I can only overtake her!"

The chase was not destined to be over very soon. Scarcely had Nancy glimpsed the other car than it turned into a side road.

"She knows I'm following her, and means to lead me a merry chase!" Nancy thought. "Her machine is slower than mine, but on the bad roads she'll have almost an even break!"

Without hesitation, she turned from the main highway. The side road was winding and narrow. Nancy dared not speed over the deep ruts lest she break a spring of her fine, new roadster. It was annoying, almost maddening, to see the other car gradually increasing the distance between them.

"At least that woman is smart!" Nancy reflected grimly. "She knows I'm on her trail and she means to get away!"

Again Nancy increased the speed. The machine roared down the highway, swinging around bends. As she approached each obscure crossroad, she blew her horn. So intent was she upon watching the car ahead of her, however, that she paid scant attention to the fact that she was covering a lot of distance. She did not realize that she was drawing near the main road.

Suddenly the highway loomed up ahead of her. A blue roadster, approaching from the right at a good clip, ran over to the wrong side of the road. Using all her strength, Nancy slammed on the foot brakes and jerked at the emergency. The other automobile swerved, though not in time.

Crash! The two cars struck, their fenders locking. Nancy's roadster went into a long skid, dragging the other automobile with it. Then, almost miraculously, both came to a standstill right side up.

Quickly, Nancy sprang out to see how much damage had been done.

"Why, Doctor Stafford!" she exclaimed in astonishment. "I hope I haven't wrecked your machine."

Although the pastor was somewhat shaken up by the accident, he smiled as he stepped from the car. A brief survey convinced him that only a little paint had been removed from one fender.

"It was all my fault," Nancy said politely. "I was pursuing another car and I didn't see you in time."

"Tut, tut, there's no damage done," the pastor assured her. "I was driving somewhat absent-mindedly and shouldn't have been over so far. Accidents will happen."

"This is the first time I ever did such a thing."

Nancy bent down to look at the axle of her own car. It had not been bent. The only evidence of the crash was a slight dent in the front fender.

However, the accident had brought to an end all hope of overtaking the strange woman. Ruefully, Nancy gazed down the road. The car had vanished.

After offering profuse apologies, she was about to take leave of the minister.

"Oh, by the way," he remarked, "I am on my way to the Blairs' estate—Jolly Folly. It has a very suggestive name, I must say."

"I just came from there," Nancy informed him. "The Blairs are away for the day."

The minister disclosed his disappointment.

"I had hoped to have a long talk with them. Since I spoke with your father I have worried about those twins. I couldn't rest if I thought they had been placed in a bad environment."

"It's very good of you to take such an interest in them," Nancy declared warmly. "Have you heard anything further from that woman who called at your home?"

She asked the question casually, not expecting an affirmative reply.

"Why, yes, I have. In truth, that is the reason I am calling upon the Blairs today."

"Did the same woman come to your house?"

"Oh, no, I should have detained her had I met her again. She telephoned. A mysterious call came from someone and I feel confident that it was she."

"How strange!"

"She asked me if I had delivered the message to your father."

"And you told her you had?"

"Yes. I explained that it was too late to carry out her wishes—that the adoption papers had been signed already."

"Did she take the news as a blow?"

"I fear so. There was a long silence as if she were completely stunned by the information. Then, before I could learn who she was or offer a word of comfort, she hung up the receiver."

"Did you try to trace the call?"

"Yes, it came from a pay station."

"Probably from some drug store," Nancy said musingly. "Did you by any chance mention that the Blairs have already removed the twins from the Selkirk Home to their own residence?"

"Why, yes, I believe I did."

Nancy said no more, yet in her mind she was convinced that the stranger who had called the pastor was the person she had been pursuing. Why had the woman made such frantic attempts to keep her identity concealed? If Nancy could speak with her for a few minutes, matters might be cleared up.

"As I mentioned, I am on my way to the Blair estate now," Doctor Stafford informed her. "A filling station man told me how to reach the place, but his directions weren't very clear."

Nancy knew that it was useless to try to overtake the fleeing woman, now that so much time had been lost.

"I am returning there myself," she told the minister. "If you care to follow me, I'll lead the way."

"Perhaps you drive too fast for me."

"I'll not go over twenty-five," Nancy promised him with a laugh. "I'm not taking chances on any more accidents today."

A few minutes later the two cars drew up before the Blairs' imposing residence. Bess was on the front lawn with the babies. She gathered from the expression on her chum's face that Nancy had failed in her attempt to overtake the mysterious woman, but she avoided asking any questions. Proudly she displayed her young charges to the kindly minister.

"As fine a pair of twins as I ever saw!" he declared. "And in my time I have baptized dozens of them."

"Oh, by the way," Nancy asked, "did you look up the names of the first twins—Ruth and Rodney?"

The minister disclosed his chagrin.

"Dear me, it completely slipped my mind. But I will do it tomorrow surely. I must ask my wife where those old records were placed."

Nancy hid her disappointment. She felt that the point she had brought up was highly important, although neither her father nor the pastor considered it significant. The delay was, however, exceedingly annoying.

Nancy was always impatient for action. Her father chided her by saying that nearly all of her worries were the result of "things not happening fast enough."

While Doctor Stafford and the girls were admiring the twins, an automobile turned into the drive. Nancy noticed it first, and thought that the Blairs were returning home.

However, as it approached, she saw that it was a much smaller car than the one owned by the theatrical couple.

A strange man sat at the wheel. He stopped the car with a jerk and sprang to the ground.

Without glancing toward Nancy or her companions, he rushed up to the front door and rang the bell officiously.

"He'll ruin the electric battery if he keeps on like that," Bess laughed. "I guess we'd better tell him the Blairs are out."

They moved forward, and the stranger turned toward them impatiently.

"Why doesn't someone answer the bell?" he demanded in annoyance. "Have all the maids gone on strike?"

"The Blairs aren't at home," Nancy informed him politely.

She was trying to make up her mind whether or not the newcomer was a traveling salesman. He did not carry a sample case or a portfolio. He was expensively dressed, and his confident manner stamped him as a person of authority.

"You say they aren't at home?" he inquired, scowling. "Now, that's a pretty how'd'do! Where've they gone?"

"I'm sure I can't say, but I saw them drive away with golf clubs."

"More than likely to the Country Club. They're always gadding about when they should be attending to business!"

"Is there a message you wish to leave?"

The man stared at Nancy; then, noticing that her face seemed unusually intelligent, he decided to state his business.

"I'm McNeery—Edwin McNeery."

As this name produced no visible effect upon Nancy, he added:

"I'm a theatrical producer—own a chain of theaters. You've heard of the McNeery shows."

"Yes, indeed," Nancy acknowledged.

"I've a good part for the Blairs in a new revue I'm putting on. I want to see them right off and I can't wait!"

"I'm afraid you must," Nancy smiled. "I have no idea when they'll return. We are taking care of their babies for them."

"Their *what?*"

For the first time, the man seemed to notice the twins. He stared at them hostilely.

"The Blairs have adopted twins from the Selkirk Home," Nancy informed him, an amused look in her eyes. "Surely you must have heard about them."

"Heard about 'em?"

Edwin McNeery raged. "If I had, you can just bet it wouldn't have been done! You're not joking?"

"No, the adoption papers have been signed."

"It's an outrage!"

The producer's face flushed angrily, and he fell to pacing the veranda. Suddenly he wheeled toward Nancy.

"They can't get away with this and work for Edwin McNeery! Those babies are going back to the Home in double-quick time!"

CHAPTER X

An Ultimatum

"And is that the message you wish me to deliver to the Blairs?" Nancy inquired, smiling.

The producer hesitated.

"Yes, tell them just that! If they expect to work for me, they must keep their minds on their business."

From his coat pocket he withdrew a thick envelope which he tapped significantly.

"I have a new contract here for them to sign. I won't have time to come back, so I'll leave it with you."

"I'll give it to the Blairs just as soon as they arrive," Nancy promised him.

"And tell them what I said about the babies, too. Back they go to the Home!"

Mr. McNeery had taken to pacing the veranda again, puffing viciously at a strong cigar.

"The Blairs won't dare go against my wishes," he fumed. "They know where their bread and butter comes from."

Although Nancy and Bess said nothing, they did not miss a word of the tirade.

"They won't dare turn down this contract,"

the producer went on to himself. "They can bluff most people but they can't bluff me! This house—the fine grounds"—his hand swept out in a disparaging gesture—"all are mortgaged to the hilt!"

Here, indeed, was news for Nancy and Bess. They listened attentively.

"Kitty and Johnny Blair have talent," McNeery went on, cooling down slightly. "I'd be the last person in the world to deny it. But they're lazy and live beyond their means. They don't like to rehearse and they're always complaining about the parts they get. I'd toss them over in a minute if they weren't able to put over their stuff!"

He ceased his pacing long enough to stare at the babies.

"I have troubles enough without adding twins! You tell the Blairs to get rid of 'em and to do it quick, too!"

"I'll acquaint them with what you say," Nancy promised.

"Well, you needn't tell them everything. Maybe I said a little more than I intended, but those people infuriate me sometimes! Just tell them about the babies—that business is business, and sentiment should be left out of it."

He thrust the long sealed envelope into her hand and turned to leave.

"You won't forget to give this contract to them, will you?"

"I'll put it in their hands as soon as they come in," Nancy assured him.

"O.K., and many thanks!"

With these words the producer hurried down the steps, flung himself into his car, and drove away.

"Well, well," Bess remarked when they were alone, "we're hearing plenty of news."

"And all of it detrimental to the Blairs. Bess, I didn't like that man, but he's refreshingly honest. I almost hope he forces the Blairs to send the babies back!"

"So do I. I've always thought an Orphan Home would be a dreadful place for children to be reared in, but I've changed my mind. Judging from the care these babies got, they're good places."

"If we can only get the twins back to the Selkirk Home, their real parents may turn up," Nancy added hopefully.

Although neither girl cared to put her feelings into words, both had grown to dislike the Blairs intensely, while their love for the twins had developed by leaps and bounds. Mr. McNeery's visit encouraged them to believe that the unfortunate situation might right itself in time.

The girls looked about for Doctor Stafford. During the conversation the minister had wandered away to inspect the grounds. They could see him down by the river.

"It's just as well he was out of hearing," Nancy commented. "He might have been offended at some of Mr. McNeery's ideas about babies."

"Here comes someone on foot, Nancy," Bess interrupted. "I wonder who it can be?"

They were not left in doubt for long. The man walked up to the place where they were standing and addressed them politely.

"I am looking for Mr. or Mrs. Blair."

"They are both out for the day," Nancy returned.

The man eyed her quizzically.

"That's what I'm always told when I call."

"But they really are away," Nancy maintained. "Is there a message I can give them?"

"Give them this."

The man thrust forward a grocery bill. The long column of figures and the huge total amazed Nancy.

"I'll see that they get it," she offered.

The collector smiled and shook his head.

"They'd only tear it up. No, I'll call again and see them in person. However, they'll get no more groceries from my firm until they've paid us what they owe. This bill has been running for months."

"Really!" Nancy murmured.

Here was more interesting news. She was learning a great deal about the financial standing of the Blairs.

"This isn't the only bill they owe—not by a long shot! I guess they think it's fashionable to keep folks waiting for their money." So saying, the man turned and walked away.

Scarcely had he vanished than the girls caught a glimpse of the cook trudging up the walk with a basket filled with food slung over her arm. Nancy hurried to assist her.

"You shouldn't carry such a heavy load," she chided.

The woman sank down in the shade of the veranda to rest.

"And who will if I don't?" she sniffed. "The butcher has refused to deliver here because the bills aren't paid. I'm sick and tired of working for such people!"

The girls helped her carry the basket to the kitchen. Returning to the veranda, they found that the Reverend Doctor Stafford had finished his tour of inspection of the grounds.

"I don't believe I'll wait for Mr. and Mrs. Blair any longer," he told them, stepping into his car. "I may call again tomorrow. Good day, and thank you."

The girls watched him drive away. Then, deciding that the twins had been out of doors long enough for one time, they carried them to the second floor.

"At least, we've given Colleen a good rest," Nancy remarked. "I hope she's feeling better by this time."

The girls gasped in surprise as they entered the nursery. Preening herself before a long mirror stood the nursemaid, arrayed in Mrs. Blair's new evening gown.

"Why, Colleen!" Nancy exclaimed reprovingly.

"Oh!"

Frantically the girl began to tug at the dress, trying to pull it off over her head.

"Wait!" Nancy warned. "Let me help you with it!"

Too late. Colleen gave a vicious pull and ripped a drape of the flimsy material. She gazed down at the long tear in horror.

"Oh, oh, see what I've done!"

"You had no right to be trying on Mrs. Blair's clothes," Bess told her sternly.

Colleen burst into tears.

"Oh, I'll be discharged now! I didn't mean to tear the dress. I didn't think it would do a bit of harm just to see how it would look on me! Oh, oh, what shall I do?"

"It doesn't do any good to cry, that's certain," Nancy said, not unkindly.

She picked up the gown and carefully examined the tear.

"Go get a needle and thread, Colleen. I believe you can mend this so it won't show."

"I can't sew."

Nancy and Bess exchanged quick glances. It seemed to them that Colleen could do nothing

useful. She had taken advantage of them by
inducing them to care for the babies while she
rested. Although they felt that she deserved
no help, the girls did not have the heart to see
her exposed to Mrs. Blair's wrath. If the actress ever were to discover that the nursemaid
had worn her gown, it was a foregone conclusion that she would discharge Colleen.

"If I mend the dress for you, will you promise never to touch Mrs. Blair's things again?"
Nancy asked her.

"Oh, Miss Drew, it's so good of you!"

"But do you promise?"

"Yes! If you'll mend the drape! I'll get
the thread."

Before Nancy had time to change her mind,
Colleen darted from the room.

"You're foolish to do it," Bess declared.

"I suppose I am," Nancy sighed, "but I hate
to see anyone in trouble."

"She brought this upon herself."

"Yes. But perhaps it will teach her a les-
son. I don't like to deceive Mrs. Blair about
the gown, but if we tell her she's certain to discharge Colleen."

With her position hanging in the balance, the
girl lost no time finding thread and needle.
She watched anxiously while Nancy labored
over the drape.

"It's a more difficult tear than I thought,"
Nancy remarked.

"Hurry!" Colleen urged impatiently, glancing at the clock. "Mrs. Blair may be home any minute now."

Nancy sewed as rapidly as she could, taking neat, tiny stitches. The flimsy material was difficult to handle.

Before she had finished, the roar of a motor car was heard on the drive. Colleen rushed to the window.

"Oh, the Blairs are coming home!" she cried in horror.

Nervously Nancy tried to stitch faster.

"I have only a little more to do."

Colleen began to wring her hands.

"They're coming into the house!" she reported from the window.

"It will take them a few minutes to remove their wraps," Nancy said.

Colleen looked about the room like a trapped animal seeking an avenue of escape.

"I must go down to the kitchen to see about the babies' supper!" she declared glibly.

Before the girls could stop her she dashed from the room.

"The little coward!" Bess exclaimed.

Nancy laughed ruefully.

"Think up something quickly, Bess, or we'll be in for a lot of explaining!"

Not until Colleen had deserted the scene had it occurred to Nancy that Mrs. Blair might blame them for the torn gown.

CHAPTER XI

A TORN GOWN

NANCY's nimble fingers stitched away, her mind actively planning some solution to the awkward situation in which she found herself and her chum.

"Quick, Bess!" She indicated the McNeery contract which they had brought to the nursery with them. It lay upon the table. "Take that envelope downstairs and waylay the Blairs! Keep them out of the nursery as long as you possibly can."

Bess snatched up the document and darted from the room.

From below a door slammed. Mr. and Mrs. Blair had entered the house, and it was plain that they were quarreling.

"Such a day!" Mrs. Blair was heard to say. "Really, Johnny, if you can't learn to play better golf you should stay at home. Imagine taking a twelve at the ninth hole! Outrageous!"

"I'd have done well enough if you hadn't kept nagging at me every minute!" came the sharp retort. "Nothing I do pleases you."

"That's because you do everything so abominably!"

"Oh, cut the dramatics!" Johnny snapped. "You're not on the stage now."

"I wish I had never married you—a cheap actor!"

The voices suddenly died down. Nancy, listening from above, guessed that the Blairs had caught sight of Bess. A moment later she heard exclamations of pleasure and knew that the contract had been given them.

Desperately Nancy sewed away on the frock. At last it was repaired. Hurrying with the gown to Mrs. Blair's bedroom, she quietly stole over to the closet and hung the dress on a vacant hook. Great as was the need for haste, she could not refrain from glancing about her.

It was such a bedroom as she had imagined the actress would have. The furniture was highly ornate and gaudy. A dressing table ladened with bottles of expensive perfumes stood near a window. Silk pillows and French dolls were everywhere. Movie magazines and cheap thrillers were strewn over the floor.

The closet was filled with elaborate gowns. Nancy had never before seen so many in the possession of one person. A special shelf had been built to accommodate the long row of shoes.

"She might be planning to open a second-hand clothing business!'' Nancy chuckled, turning from the room. ''No wonder the Blairs owe the butcher and baker.''

She stole into the nursery just in time to avoid questioning. Bess was coming up the stairs with the actor and his wife. They had not yet opened the sealed contract.

Evidently the sight of their adopted parents was not agreeable to the twins, for no sooner had Mr. and Mrs. Blair set foot in the nursery than Jay and Janet began to cry. Nancy rushed over to quiet them.

''Now, what's the matter?'' Kitty demanded irritably. ''Every time we step into the nursery they start that bellowing!''

''They've been good babies all day.''

''Humph! It's hard to believe. They'll drive me crazy with their screaming.''

Mr. Blair stepped forward, and before Nancy could intervene, had snatched Janet from her crib.

''I know how to stop 'em. Here, kid, your daddy will teach you to step!''

As he roughly pulled the child about in the semblance of a dance, her screams grew more piercing. When he tried to make Janet turn a somersault, Nancy could endure the sight no longer.

''Let me have her,'' she pleaded. ''If you and Mrs. Blair will just leave me alone with the twins for a little while I'll quiet them.''

"We wanted to hear what McNeery had to say about the contract," Mrs. Blair protested.

"I'll come downstairs and discuss it with you in just a minute."

Almost without their realizing it, Nancy hustled the pair out of the room. With the cause of the disturbance removed, she soon had the youngsters quiet again.

Colleen, believing that she would not be found out, had returned to the nursery.

"Did Mrs. Blair see the dress?" she asked fearfully.

"I hardly think she's gone to her room yet," Nancy returned coldly. "It wasn't very sporting of you to run away as you did, Colleen."

The girl had the grace to look ashamed.

"I—I just thought of something I had to tell the cook."

Nancy let the excuse pass. Telling the maid to remain with the children, she descended to the first floor where Bess and the Blairs were awaiting her in the den. They had opened the contract and were studying it eagerly.

They began to besiege Nancy with questions. Had McNeery dropped any hint as to how badly he was in need of their services? Did she think he would offer more money if they refused to sign?

"He did say one thing," Nancy reported, watching their faces closely. "It was about the twins."

"I knew he'd want them!" Kitty exclaimed. "We can make him pay plenty for their services."

Nancy was forced to disillusion her.

"He doesn't want the twins. In fact, he said that they must be sent back to the Home!"

Kitty looked surprised, but no other emotion was mirrored in her face.

"Why should I send the babies back just to please him?"

"That's up to you, of course," Nancy said smoothly. "He intimated, however, that unless you did so he would not use you or your husband in his new revue."

"I like his nerve! Imagine telling us what to do!"

"Maybe we'd better follow his advice," Johnny suggested nervously.

Kitty withered him with a glance.

"We'll do nothing in haste, that's certain. I must think this thing out."

Kitty told nothing of what was passing through her mind. Presently she turned to her husband and smiled.

"We'll not be in a hurry to sign this paper, Johnny. I know McNeery, and he'll not be so high-handed if we keep him in suspense a while."

Some plan was brewing in the actress's mind, Nancy felt confident. Whether or not the woman meant to give up the twins she had no way of guessing. If Kitty should cling stubbornly to the babies, then Nancy would disclose a scheme of her own which had gradually been taking shape in her mind. If, she reasoned, she could locate the mysterious woman whom she believed to be the babies' mother, it might be possible for her to induce the Blairs to engage the stranger as a nurse.

"It will be only a matter of time until Colleen will be discharged," Nancy reflected. "She really isn't capable of caring for the twins. Now, if I can locate their real mother they'll receive the tender care they need."

The tinkle of the telephone broke in upon her thoughts. Mrs. Blair arose to answer it. Her voice became smooth as velvet as she learned that it was the society editor of a daily paper who was calling.

"You wish a picture of me with the babies?" she purred into the transmitter. "How nice! Your staff photographer will call tomorrow? Yes, I'll be here. I daren't go far from the house, now that I have the darling babies to watch over, you know."

When the conversation ended, Nancy and Bess announced that they must return home. They were thoroughly disgusted with Mrs. Blair and her hypocritical ways.

"We've had a busy day," Bess remarked wearily as they drove away.

"Yes, but I'm disappointed because that

stranger managed to slip away from me. Everything would work out splendidly if I could only get her installed as the children's nurse."

"So that's your scheme? I knew you were mulling over something."

"Executing the plan won't be easy. I have no idea where to find that woman."

"Too bad that Doctor Stafford had to get in your way today."

"Yes, but I really was to blame partly."

"You didn't get the license number of the woman's car, did you?"

"No, I couldn't draw up close enough for that. I suppose now I've lost her for good."

"If she actually is the mother, I'm sure she'll come back," Bess declared hopefully.

The girls discussed the case pro and con until they reached River Heights. There Nancy dropped Bess off at her home, promising to call the following afternoon.

She looked forward to having a long talk with her father at dinner. Greatly to her disappointment, however, she found a note stating that he had been called out of town on business and would not be home until late that night.

At breakfast the next morning there was no opportunity for Nancy to bring up the subject, for Mr. Drew was in a hurry to reach the Municipal Court.

When she tried to tell Hannah about the twins, the housekeeper assumed a disdainful attitude. She was still afraid that her young mistress might wish to bring the babies home with her.

"You take my advice, Nancy, and don't be meddling in other folks' affairs," she warned. "Mysteries are all right—but children are a different matter."

Nancy was glad when the time came for her to call upon Bess, for she knew her chum would enjoy discussing the case with her. A dilapidated car stood before the Marvin residence as Nancy pulled up to the curb. Before she could alight, a boyish voice greeted her from the porch.

"Hello, Nancy, don't bump into my new runabout."

"George Fayne! What are you doing here?"

Nancy rushed up the walk to greet the girl, a cousin of Bess, and a chum of long standing. She was as boyish as her name.

"Oh, just prowling around. Lucky I came, because Bess has been hinting that you've dug up another mystery."

"We're working on one," Nancy laughed.

"Bess won't tell me a thing. She says you'll have to do all the explaining."

"All right. Let's go inside."

While seated in the comfortable living room

of the Marvin home, Bess and Nancy quickly told George all that had occurred at Jolly Folly.

"Holding out on me, weren't you?" accused George.

"We didn't mean to," Nancy laughed. "We've simply been so busy we haven't done anything except look after babies."

"What about the mysterious telegrams, telephone calls, and adventurous chases over the country!" George enumerated. "I'm downright peeved that I wasn't let in on the secret."

"But you shall be from now on," Bess declared.

"I'm glad of that. By the way, Nancy, what did that mysterious woman look like?"

"She wore a gray suit and a black felt hat with a red quill in it. She was of average height."

"Gray, did you say?" George asked quickly.

"Yes. Doctor Stafford talked to her. He said she had a very musical voice."

George looked up quickly.

"Then she's the same one!" she cried.

"Who is?" Nancy demanded tensely. "Have you seen the woman?"

"I'm sure of it."

"Where? Oh, hurry and tell us!" Bess urged.

"In the drug store this morning. I was having a chocolate soda."

"What was the woman doing? How did she act?" Nancy cried impatiently.

"Like any other woman who was interested in baby food."

"Baby food!" Nancy and Bess cried in one voice. "Did she buy it?"

"I think the druggist gave her several sample cans. I didn't pay much attention to it, to tell you the truth. I just remember that they had a long discussion about the merits and demerits of each can."

"What drug store was it?" Nancy demanded.

"Jackson's."

Nancy started for the door, Bess directly behind her. George caught up her béret and hurried after them.

"Say, have you girls lost your minds?"

"We're going to the drug store to find out more about that woman!" Nancy called to her.

"I've told you all there is to tell."

"The druggist may know who she is. We'll question him, at an any rate."

The girls piled into Nancy's car and drove three blocks to Jackson's Drug Store where they ordered ice cream. While they were eating, they sought to draw the druggist into conversation.

Adroitly Nancy questioned the man, but he knew very little about the strange woman. He admitted having given her several sample cans of baby food, but whether or not they were for her own children he could not say. Neither did he know her name.

Noting that the man was growing suspicious of so many questions, the girls gave up trying to learn anything further. Hurriedly they finished their ice cream. Nancy then gathered up the checks, and the girls arose to leave the table.

At that moment the outside door opened. Nancy glanced up casually to see who had entered. Quickly she pulled her chums back into the shelter of a large sign.

"It's Rodney!" Bess murmured.

"Let's wait and see what he wants," Nancy whispered. "If we keep quiet he won't look over this way."

The chauffeur wore street clothes and a wide-brimmed hat which was pulled low over his eyes. He glanced carefully about the room as if to make certain that no customers were about. Then, gliding swiftly toward the counter where the pharmacist was standing, he bent over and whispered something.

The three girls were bewildered by the chauffeur's secretive manner. They were even more stunned by what followed.

"Don't give them that, man!" the druggist shouted, greatly excited. "You'll kill the babies!"

CHAPTER XII

RODNEY'S QUEER ACTIONS

RODNEY murmured something to the druggist which Nancy and her friends could not hear. However, not an action escaped their keen eyes as the old pharmacist went into the back room. While he was gone, Rodney moved nervously about.

The druggist returned a moment later with a package of baby food and a bottle of medicine. Rodney quickly paid for the articles and left the store.

"Do you suppose he bought that baby food and medicine for Jay and Janet?" Bess questioned anxiously.

"It looks that way," Nancy agreed.

"But why did the druggist say the things he did? It worries me."

Nancy was troubled, too. She felt at a loss to explain Rodney's actions. However, the incident confirmed her suspicion that he had a secret interest in the twins.

"I believe Colleen would call us if the babies were seriously ill," she said thoughtfully.

After bidding her friends good-bye, Nancy

went home and lingered about the yard, half
expecting a message from Jolly Folly. When
none came she felt relieved, yet at the same
time anxious. To ease her mind, she put
through a telephone call of her own.

"No, the babies aren't ill," Colleen assured
her, "but Mr. and Mrs. Blair are in an awful
state. They can't decide what to do about
the twins."

Two days elapsed before Nancy saw or heard
anything from Jolly Folly.

On the morning of the third day, while at
breakfast, she opened the newspaper. A large
picture of Mrs. Blair and the twins met her
eyes. The photo revealed her holding the babies in her arms, gazing upon them raptur-
ously.

With an exclamation of annoyance, Nancy
handed the sheet over to her father.

"How disgusting and hypocritical that is,"
said Nancy in a tone that betrayed her true
feelings.

"It seems to come natural for Mrs. Blair,"
Mr. Drew smiled, studying the pose. "Yesterday I was reading of a case quite different. A
noted actress had given up her career because
she preferred to devote herself to her home and
children."

Nancy turned over the sheets to the classi-
fied advertisements section, and scanned the
columns from force of habit. One notice stood

out from the rest, and immediately caught her eye.

"Listen to this, Father," she exclaimed. " 'Wanted—Responsible woman to act as babies' nurse. Experienced only. Apply at the Selkirk Babies' Foundling Home.' "

"You're not going after the job, are you, Nancy?"

"No, Father. But it gave me an idea!"

"What sort of an idea?"

"A good one, I hope! Doesn't it occur to you to wonder why there is a vacancy for a nurse at the Home?"

"Can't say it does, Nancy. But immediately after breakfast is the hour I am usually half asleep."

"Oh, please try to be serious! I really think I have a worth-while hunch! You recall this mysterious woman we've been hearing so much about."

"I hear about her every morning at the table," Mr. Drew returned, trying hard not to smile.

"And I'm afraid you'll hear about her until I learn who she is," Nancy said gaily. "Father, it occurred to me that possibly she has been employed at the Selkirk Home, and while there cared for the twins. Then, when they were taken away, she left, too!"

Mr. Drew's face grew sober as he meditated over this theory.

"That's not in the realm of the impossible. It seems to explain why the woman suddenly turned up to protest the adoption."

"My theory exactly! While the babies were under her care, she was content to allow them to remain at the Home. I believe I'll run out there today and see what I can find out. That is, if you'll give me an advance on my next week's allowance so that I can buy gasoline."

Mr. Drew stripped several bills from his wallet.

"Here you are. We'll charge this item to the expense account of the Blair baby case!"

Nancy did not want to make the twenty-five-mile trip alone. As Bess and George were always eager for adventure, she called them up, and was overjoyed to learn that they would be ready in half an hour.

By ten o'clock the girls were speeding toward Selkirk, located on the Muskoka River below River Heights. The route took them past Jolly Folly.

"Let's drop in for just a minute and look at the babies," Bess suggested wistfully. "George hasn't seen them yet."

Nancy was more than willing. Despite Colleen's telephone message, she did not feel entirely at ease about the twins. It was actually a relief to see the nursemaid out in the garden with the perambulator as they drove up.

"I guess everyone worries about Jay and

Janet," Colleen laughed, displaying her charges for George's benefit. "Rodney is the worst one, though."

Nancy and her friends listened intently to her next words.

"He thinks I don't know how to feed babies, I suppose!" Colleen went on, tossing her head contemptuously. "The idea of a chauffeur trying to tell me things like that! He'd give the kids automobile grease if he had his way!"

"Automobile grease!" Bess ejaculated, horrified.

"Well, maybe not quite that bad," Colleen laughed, "but some stuff out of cans that looks just as bad to eat."

"Prepared baby food," Nancy suggested.

"Yes, some he bought at the store and from a woman pedlar."

"Oh," Nancy observed alertly, "did a woman pedlar stop here with some baby foods?"

"What did she look like?" Bess interposed.

"I didn't spend much time looking at her, but Rodney did, all right. I saw him talking with her for nearly half an hour. When he came back to the house he carried an armful of baby foods!"

Unknown to Colleen, the chauffeur had overheard her remark as he was rounding the corner of the house. Nancy and her chums tried to warn the girl with signs, but to no avail.

Rodney stepped forward, ready to defend himself.

"You may laugh all you like about the baby foods," he snapped, "but you'll notice that since they began using them the twins look better!"

"They do have more color in their cheeks," Bess observed.

"The babies haven't been getting the proper care and attention," Rodney continued heatedly. "That's why I interested myself in their food."

Colleen's face flushed angrily.

"I suppose you think you're a specialist, Mr. Brown!"

"At least, when I don't know what to do I'm wise enough to consult someone who does!"

Nancy glanced curiously at the man, wondering if that was why he had gone to the pharmacist at Jackson's Drug Store.

"You'd do better if you'd attend to your automobile and let me look after the twins," Colleen said crossly.

"You neglect them while you go running around with that red-haired young man of yours," the chauffeur said accusingly. "The babies would have been poisoned if you had gone on with the silly idea of feeding that the Blairs insisted upon."

A feeling of intense relief came over Nancy as she heard this declaration. She recalled the druggist's strange exclamation, when Rodney had shown him something:

"Don't give them that, man, for you'll kill them!"

She was now of the opinion that Rodney had brought a sample of the baby food from the Blair household to the pharmacist for a chemical analysis. It was good to know that the chauffeur's intentions had been of the best.

"I think he knows what he is talking about," Nancy told Colleen. "You should take his advice about the baby foods."

Colleen tossed her head impatiently.

"He only knows what that pedlar woman told him."

"What did she look like?" Nancy asked again. "Do you remember how she was dressed?"

"In gray, I believe. He said something about red trimming on her hat."

Neither Nancy nor her friends disclosed that this information was important, though they were inwardly thrilled. However, it was impossible to learn more of the woman's appearance from Colleen, so they dared not jump to the conclusion that the pedlar and the individual whom George had seen in the drug store were one and the same person.

While they were talking, the front door opened and the Blairs, dressed in their flashiest clothes, and accompanied by Edwin

McNeery, emerged. They paused to greet the girls.

"We're so sorry to run away just when you are arriving," Kitty gushed, "but Mr. McNeery insists that we go out for a drive with him."

The producer smiled blandly. He seemed in fine spirits, but Nancy surmised that this was largely put on. Despite his boastful words, he really needed the Blairs in his new show, and their delay in signing the contract was causing him much anxiety.

She could see the papers sticking out from his coat pocket. Undoubtedly, McNeery's plan was to take the couple away for a day of pleasure. Then, when they were in a gay, light-hearted mood, he would bring out the contract for them to sign.

Mrs. Blair bent over the baby carriage for an instant. As she did so, Nancy saw a scowl on the producer's face. McNeery made no comment—his very silence was oppressive. He meant to do as he wished with the twins.

After the group had driven away Nancy stood gazing after the automobile.

"It's a shame," she murmured to herself. "Neither McNeery nor the Blairs have the slightest interest in the welfare of Jay and Janet! Unless someone takes a hand in it, their happiness will be sacrificed for the silly careers of their foster parents!"

CHAPTER XIII

Mistaken Identity

"What are you saying, Nancy?" George demanded.

Nancy started. She had not realized that she was speaking aloud.

"Nothing. I was just mumbling a little to myself."

Colleen had not heard Nancy's observation about McNeery or the Blairs. She casually remarked:

"Mr. McNeery doesn't like children."

"Why do you say that?" Nancy questioned alertly.

"Oh, you can tell by the way he looks at them. I guess he was pretty mean to his wife, too."

"Then he is married?"

"He was. I heard Mrs. Blair say that his wife left him because he was so heartless."

Colleen prepared to wheel the twins into the house. Nancy and her friends recalled that if they were to accomplish anything at Selkirk, they must be on their way soon. They hastily bade good-bye to the nursemaid and drove away.

"Well, our call was worth while," Nancy commented, as the girls sped down the road. "Every time we visit Jolly Folly we add to our general supply of information."

"I'm getting hopelessly entangled in clues," Bess declared. "What do you make of Rodney, Nancy?"

"I think that he seems to be interested in the babies' welfare instead of their ruination!"

"If we have any luck at the Selkirk Home today, things may clear up a little for us," Nancy said. "I'm as much interested in the mysterious woman as I am in Rodney."

It was nearly noon, and the crisp air had given the girls a keen appetite. Glimpsing an attractive little inn by the side of the road, they decided to stop there for luncheon.

One o'clock found them on their way once more, and shortly thereafter they drove into Selkirk. A friendly policeman directed them to the impressive-looking Foundling Home which stood upon a high bluff overlooking the Muskoka River.

"It looks like a nice place," George commented, surveying the expanse of well-kept lawn. "At least the children have lots of room in which to play."

The girls walked slowly toward the main entrance.

"Bess and I will wait outside," George proposed. "The grounds look rather attractive."

"You won't need us, anyway," Bess added.

"I may be in there a long time," Nancy told them.

"Stay as long as you like," Bess told her. "We'll walk about the grounds until you've finished your errand."

Nancy continued along up the walk to the front entrance of the rambling, red brick structure. She caught herself wondering in which of the many wings little Jay and Janet had been housed.

The door was slightly ajar, so she decided to enter. She found herself in a barren, wide hall, immaculately clean. At the far end was a desk at which sat a middle-aged woman in a white uniform. Nancy walked up to her.

"I should like to speak to the matron, if I may," she said politely.

She was conscious of the attendant's curious scrutiny.

"Mrs. Roberts is busy at present. I shall tell her you are here."

After Nancy had given her name, the attendant escorted her to a nearby seat and left the hall. Returning a few minutes later, she busied herself at the desk again. As time passed and no one appeared, Nancy grew impatient.

She was on the verge of speaking to the attendant once more, when the hall door opened.

Nancy arose to meet an efficient-looking

woman with kind eyes and snow-white hair.
Mrs. Roberts seemed to encompass the situation in one keen glance. She did not give the
River Heights girl an opportunity to state her
errand.

"I am sorry to have kept you waiting—dou-
bly so, now that I see you are far too young!"

"Too young?" Nancy stammered, not under-
standing what the matron meant.

"Yes, we must have an older, more experienced person. It would only be a waste of your
time and mine for me to interview you."

Nancy now gathered that she had been mistaken for someone else. With much amuse-
ment she recalled the advertisement she had
read in the morning paper. The matron
thought that she was applying for the position
of nurse at the Home.

"I am not looking for work," Nancy assured
her with a smile. "I came to talk to you about
an entirely different matter."

She then introduced herself, explaining that
she was the daughter of Carson Drew. The
matron was familiar with the name, for the attorney had called upon her a number of times
in a legal capacity. She was very profuse in
her apologies.

"A girl telephoned this morning saying she
was coming here to apply for the position,"
the matron explained. "Naturally, when I saw
you I thought you were she."

Mrs. Roberts led the way to her private office at the rear of the building, overlooking the grounds. She listened attentively while Nancy explained that she had come to the Home, hoping to find out something about a woman she thought might be employed in the capacity of nurse.

"What is her name?"

Nancy was forced to admit that she did not know.

"Can you describe her?"

Nancy gave the description which had been told her by Reverend Stafford. At first the matron looked puzzled; then her face lighted up again.

"A musical voice, you say? And she was dark and slender?"

"Yes," Nancy nodded eagerly. "Does she work here?"

"She did. However, she left our employ a short time ago. A few days, in fact."

Nancy scarcely could hide her elation. This information coincided perfectly with her theory that the mysterious woman had left the Home when the twins were taken away.

"Then the position you wish to fill here is the one this nurse vacated?" Nancy probed.

"Yes, we were sorry to see her go, for she was one of our most devoted and efficient employees. She loved babies."

"May I ask why she left?"

"She refused to give her reason. I noted that she seemed distressed about something. Family troubles, more than likely."

Nancy leaned forward eagerly.

"Tell me, did this take place about the time that the twins were adopted by a family named Blair?"

The question startled Mrs. Roberts.

"Now that I think of it, the change in her manner appeared then. She resigned the very day the twins were taken from our Home!"

Nancy's eyes danced with excitement. She was ready now to ask the most important question of all.

"Can you tell me the nurse's name, Mrs. Roberts?"

"Certainly. Ruth Brown."

Nancy almost leaped from her chair. Her father had said he did not believe that there could be any connection between the twins Reverend Stafford had baptized and Jay and Janet. How justly proud she would be to report this evidence!

Rodney's last name was Brown, too. Was it mere coincidence, or would something definite evolve from the similarity in names? Then again, the chauffeur might be one of the twins the minister had christened!

At this point in her speculating, Nancy's face clouded. She recalled that Rodney had been seen talking to the pedlar woman. Had he known that she was his sister, his actions would have betrayed him surely. Was the woman actually the same person who had served as nurse at the Home? The description as to appearance tallied, but other points seemed at variance.

Nancy was becoming submerged in clues.

"I'll think it all out later," she told herself. "Just now I must glean every bit of information I can."

"Miss Brown was devoted to Jay and Janet always," the matron explained. "I had noticed it, of course, yet it never occurred to me until this moment to connect her resignation with the adoption."

"Did Miss Brown say anything of her plans when she left here?"

"No, she did not mention where she was going. I can tell you nothing of her family, either."

Mrs. Roberts frowned slightly.

"As a usual thing, we do not employ persons without asking for a complete record of their experience and background. In Miss Brown's case we made an exception, for she was a wonderful nurse."

Obviously the matron had told all that she knew of Ruth Brown, yet Nancy was not ready to leave. She wanted to hear the story of how Jay and Janet had been found.

"They weren't 'basket babies' in the usual

sense of the word," Mrs. Roberts smiled. "They came to us in a far more startling way."

"By 'basket babies,' I suppose you mean those deposited upon doorsteps," Nancy remarked.

"Yes, a great many children come to us in that way. The doorbell rings. A nurse answers it, only to find a basket deposited on the doorstep with a note attached to it. Usually it reads, 'Please be good to my baby.' "

"And do the mothers ever come back for them?"

"Occasionally. But more often they do not. Poor things! Usually they have no money with which to support a child, and nothing to offer it."

The matron lapsed into a thoughtful silence. Nancy probed her gently by saying:

"You were speaking of the twins."

"Oh, yes, their case is different, I feel sure. They were found shortly after a storm—one of the worst we have ever experienced in this locality. The children came to us not in a basket, but in a boat!"

"A boat! How strange!"

"Yes, they were picked up by some young woman and brought here. We have kept them ever since."

"Where were the babies found?" Nancy persisted.

"Floating in a boat at the river's edge, as

far as we can figure out. I've forgotten the details of the story—they were minor."

Nancy inwardly disagreed as to the details being of minor import.

"During the time that the twins were in your care, did the mother ever communicate with you?"

"Never. At first I thought that the parents might be located, but they failed to appear."

Mrs. Roberts glanced at the wall clock somewhat pointedly. She was a very busy person, already having devoted more time to the interview than she should have.

"Just one thing more," Nancy said quickly as the matron arose. "May I see the records pertaining to the twins?"

The request was not to Mrs. Roberts' liking. She had very little time, and it was a rule of the Home never to open the books of record to casual visitors.

"It's really quite irregular, Miss Drew," she said.

"It means everything to me to see the entries," Nancy told her earnestly. "I am trying to trace the children's parentage."

The matron debated the matter a moment.

"Very well, you may see the records, though I assure you it will be a waste of time on your part."

Mrs. Roberts rang a small bell on her desk. When an attendant appeared, she ordered that the book under discussion be brought to her office.

"I am sorry I cannot take the time to aid you in finding the particulars you desire, Miss Drew," she said regretfully. "I must inspect the wards before dinner. I am late now."

Nancy thanked her for the assistance she had given, and surveyed the huge book spread out on the desk before her.

Items were made by date, she noted. By computing the age of the twins, she was able to guess within a few weeks of the day they had been brought to the Selkirk Home. She thumbed over innumerable pages without result.

Then, as she was beginning to despair of ever finding the notation she was seeking, she saw it standing out before her eyes.

"Twin babies, found on Muskoka River in a boat by Miss Brown."

"Does it mean Ruth Brown, I wonder?" she reflected. "This is the most important revelation yet! I must ask the matron about it."

She closed the huge book with a snap, and arose. Moving past the window, she suddenly paused, transfixed.

A slender, dark woman with a heavy suitcase was hurrying down the walk, leaving the grounds by the back way. She wore a gray suit and a black felt hat with a red quill. *It was Ruth Brown!*

CHAPTER XIV

A CHASE OVERLAND

"SHE's heading for the railroad station, I believe!" Nancy told herself, glimpsing the steel tracks which, far in the distance, ran parallel to the grounds of the Selkirk Home. "Maybe I can catch her!"

To the amazement of several attendants nearby, she darted from the office and fairly flew through the halls. Frantically she looked about for her chums. They had wandered to the far corners of the grounds.

"Bess! George!" she called. "Hurry!"

The girls moved toward her with provoking indolence. It was not until she beckoned to them excitedly that they hastened their steps. Nancy had the motor of her car started by the time they came up.

"What's the hurry?" George asked in surprise. "What happened?"

"I'll explain everything as we go along," Nancy said tersely. "Get in, quick!"

The girls obeyed with alacrity, for they realized now that something was afoot. As they shot down a side street leading to the railway station, Nancy indicated the fleeing woman who could be seen some distance ahead of them.

"Keep your eye on her!" she directed. "It's Ruth Brown, the mysterious person we've been seeking. We must overtake her!"

Since Nancy was driving and the woman was on foot, to catch up to her appeared to be a simple matter. However, the girls had not counted upon a long bridge and a double-decked truck which was hauling cars from a factory. The truck reached the bridge first and Nancy was forced to crawl along behind it.

"There should be a law against such vehicles!" George fumed. "That truck is just four times the average length."

Nancy made no response, for she was watching Ruth Brown. The woman turned in at the railway station and was lost to view.

"We'll get up to her, all right," Bess said confidently. "She probably went in to buy a ticket."

Scarcely fifty yards beyond the bridge, at a point where another road joined the street, glared a warning sign.

"Detour!" it read.

"This is maddening!" Nancy exclaimed impatiently, swinging the car into the only clear road. "If we lose sight of that woman, all my plans will be thwarted."

The train came thundering into the station while the girls were still some distance from it. As Nancy brought the automobile to a quivering halt in the parking space alongside the depot, the last of the passengers were entering the coaches.

"There she is!" George cried.

Nancy caught a glimpse of Ruth Brown disappearing into the car. Her suitcase was handed up after her.

Nancy flung herself out of the automobile, intending to board the train herself. But she was too late. It began to move, rapidly picking up speed.

"Don't try to board!" Bess called frantically, fearful lest Nancy recklessly might attempt it.

"There goes Ruth Brown again," George groaned. "Such luck!"

Nancy lost no time in bemoaning the situation. She turned and ran into the station, but was back again in an instant, hurling herself into the driver's seat.

"That woman bought a ticket to River Heights!" she informed them tensely. "Are you girls game for a speedy ride?"

"Let's go!" George urged. "We can race the train!"

Bess was far from eager to take such a reckless drive, but she said nothing.

The road to River Heights was unusually

straight and smooth. For the greater part of
the way the pavement ran parallel with the
railroad tracks. Nancy had counted upon
these factors.

She drove fast upon the heels of the retreat-
ing train. As Nancy pressed deeper upon the
accelerator, the distance slowly decreased.

"This is some ride!" George screamed into
the wind, which tore by like a hurricane.

Bess gripped the edge of her seat. She had
never ridden so fast before in all her life.

Nancy leaned low over the wheel, her eyes
fastened upon the ribbon of road ahead. Little
by little they were gaining on the train. Trees
and telephone poles whizzed by.

"The salesman told me this car was built
for speed," Nancy murmured grimly. "Now
I know he was right."

River Heights loomed up in the distance.
The train whistled for the crossing.

Nancy was now racing even. The girls
thought the engineer was waving them on; but
as the train whistled several sharp, shrill
blasts, they suddenly realized that the train-
men were trying to warn them of the crossing.

"Slow down!" Bess screamed. "Don't try
to cross ahead of the train! I'd rather lose
that woman than my life!"

Nancy had not forgotten the crossing. She
had carefully calculated her speed and felt
that she had ample time to make it. However,

even for the sake of overtaking Ruth Brown, she would not risk her life nor that of her friends.

She brought the car to a grinding halt as they watched the train rumble by. The River Heights station was just around the bend. The train slowed down for it, giving Nancy an opportunity to make up for the time she had lost at the crossing.

"We're in time!" Bess cried joyfully, as they drove into the gravel parking space adjoining the station. "The passengers are just alighting!"

Eagerly they surveyed those who stepped from the train. Ruth Brown was one of the last to leave.

"So she did come here!" cried Bess.

"I'm going to speak to her!" Nancy announced.

She hurried forward and reached the woman just as she picked up her suitcase from the station platform.

"Miss Brown, I believe?"

The woman glanced up, startled.

"Why, yes, that is my name. I don't believe I know you."

"I am Nancy Drew," the girl returned, watching her companion closely. "Carson Drew's daughter."

"Oh!"

The telltale blood rushed to Ruth Brown's

face. Nancy was sure then that it was she who had sent the telegram. She drew the woman to a secluded corner of the station where passers-by could not overhear their conversation.

"Father and I are your friends, Miss Brown," she said gently. "Please don't be frightened."

The woman laughed.

"Did I look so? I didn't mean to. I suppose I have a great deal to explain."

"It would simplify matters if you would do so," Nancy said kindly. "Father and I are doing everything possible to untangle the unfortunate adoption of the Blair twins. We need your coöperation."

At mention of the twins, Ruth Brown's face became a study. Impulsively, she gripped Nancy's wrist.

"Oh, can't they be saved from those dreadful people?"

"She *is* the babies' mother!" Nancy thought with conviction. Aloud she said, "If you will help us, I think matters perhaps can be righted."

"Oh, I'll do anything you suggest if it's in my power."

Nancy nodded sympathetically.

"You were their nurse at the Selkirk Foundling Home, weren't you?"

Ruth Brown laughed nervously.

"I see I have no secrets from you, Miss Drew."

"I wish you would tell me your story."

"There isn't much to tell. It's true I was the babies' nurse."

"You found the babies in the first place, didn't you?"

"Yes." The woman made the confession unwillingly. "I loved the children at first sight. I wanted them for my own, but I couldn't afford to keep them. I am very poor."

Her eyes dropped, as if she were conscious of the shabby suit, the old felt hat, the worn purse. Her suitcase, too, was of poor quality and much worn. The wages of a nurse at an orphan home were small.

"I placed the twins in the Home," Miss Brown continued in a low tone. "I felt I had to be near them, so I secured a position as their nurse."

"And when they left, did you leave, too?"

"Yes, Mrs. Roberts failed to tell me that the babies were to be adopted until the very last minute. I was away from the Home when the Blairs first called."

"It was a shock to you to lose the twins, wasn't it?"

"To such people as the Blairs—yes. I was much upset. I know now that I shouldn't have sent the telegram to your father."

"I am very glad that you did," Nancy told her sympathetically.

"In my anxiety over the babies, I left the Home without taking any of my clothes," the woman explained. "That was why I went back today."

During the recital, Nancy had been studying Ruth Brown's face. She was more than half convinced that the woman was the real mother of the children. The nurse's distress over the adoption seemed to confirm this suspicion.

"It's good of you to take such an interest in the case," she continued wearily, reaching down for her suitcase, "but I've come to the conclusion that nothing can be done for the babies. The papers have been signed."

Nancy was unwilling to lose track of the nurse so soon.

"I wish you would talk with my father," she urged. "Why not come to the house with me now?"

Miss Brown hesitated.

"Father may be able to think of some legal way in which to wrest the twins from the Blairs. Do come!" begged Nancy.

"If you really want me to, I will."

Nancy led the way to the car where she introduced the gaping George and Bess to Miss Brown. The girls climbed into the rumble-seat, and bade the young woman good-bye at their respective homes.

Nancy, her father and Miss Brown had a long talk at the Drew residence. The attorney could glean no further information from the nurse. However, she told him a straight-forward story, never varying in a single detail from her first account.

Nancy had hoped that her father might think of some way in which to aid the unfortunate woman. Although the lawyer plainly had Miss Brown's interests at heart, he was devoid of ideas as to how he might assist her in the matter.

Nancy took but little part in the conversation, for she was thinking. Slowly a plan began to evolve in her mind. Excusing herself, she ran to the telephone and called the Jolly Folly estate. She was relieved when the maid told her that Kitty Blair was at home.

"I've been having the most dreadful time," the actress wailed before the girl had an opportunity to speak. "Colleen has run off on a date with her friend and the twins are screaming their heads off!"

This was the very opening Nancy wanted. With an eloquence which surprised herself, she convinced Mrs. Blair that she needed an extra nurse, one especially trained to care for babies.

"I know just such a person, too," she concluded. "A wonderful nurse who has had years of experience."

"Send her out and I'll interview her," the

actress said. "At least, she can't be any worse than Colleen."

With a delighted chuckle, Nancy hung up the receiver. She felt that everything was working out as she had planned. The babies were assured of an excellent nurse, Ruth Brown would be happy to have them in her care again, and peace would descend upon the Blair household.

"If Ruth Brown really is the twins' mother, she'll be unspeakably happy to take charge of them!" she thought.

Returning to the study, Nancy quickly mentioned the offer Mrs. Blair had made.

"I am confident she will employ you, Miss Brown, if you will call at the estate tomorrow."

Mr. Drew nodded approvingly. He felt that Nancy had found an easy way out of an awkward situation.

Only Miss Brown looked downcast.

"Why, can't you take the position?" Nancy questioned, as the woman remained silent.

"I'm sorry, I wish I could. I love the babies as if they were my own, but nothing could induce me to work at Jolly Folly!"

Nancy saw all her plans completely frustrated. Her theories, too. In refusing the offer, Miss Brown had made it evident that she was not the mother of the twins.

The parents of Jay and Janet still remained a mystery.

CHAPTER XV

A Plan Disrupted

"Who in the world can this woman be?" Nancy asked herself in bewilderment. "If she isn't the mother of the twins, why is she so interested in them?"

Carson Drew likewise was puzzled at Miss Brown's refusal.

"If you don't accept the position, I'm afraid the babies will suffer," Nancy said sadly. "The nurse Mrs. Blair now has is absolutely incompetent."

The woman twisted her handkerchief nervously. She seemed torn between emotions.

"I wish I could accept the position. I'll think it over."

"Good!" Mr. Drew approved. "Where can we reach you?"

"I'll come back here," the woman said hastily.

"Do so in two days, then," Nancy suggested. "At this same hour."

Regretfully, she accompanied the woman to the door.

"Do you think we'll ever see her again,

Father?" asked Nancy, returning to Mr. Drew.

"I think we will," the lawyer responded thoughtfully. "She doesn't strike me as the sort of person to break a promise."

Nancy had no intention of remaining idle for the next two days. The following morning she visited Jolly Folly with the express purpose of questioning Rodney.

When he could not be found around the house she searched the garage. She discovered him sitting on a bench behind the building, absorbed in a letter which he was writing. He hastily thrust the paper into his pocket as she came up to him.

"A beautiful day," Nancy remarked casually. "Do you mind if I sit beside you? The view of the river is excellent from here."

The chauffeur obligingly made room for her on the bench. Nancy tried in vain to draw him into a cheerful conversation. Rodney gazed moodily toward the gleaming waters.

"Some days I feel like going down there and jumping in!"

"Why, Rodney!" Nancy exclaimed, shocked by the sentiment. "How can you say such a thing?"

"You'd say it too if you'd gone through what I have."

"The war, you mean?" Nancy asked gently.

"The war and other things. I was gassed.

Look at me now! A shadow of my former self. Look at this nose! Twisted out of shape.''

"You're far more conscious of your appearance than other people are, I'm sure, Rodney."

The chauffeur laughed harshly.

"My own relatives wouldn't recognize me—if I could find them!"

Nancy sat up very straight at this.

"If you could find them?" she repeated softly. "Then you have lost your family?"

The man inclined his head gloomily.

"I had a sister once—a twin. We were separated and I've never been able to find her. I haven't tried lately because she'd hate to see me the way I am now."

"What was her name?" Nancy asked, scarcely daring to hope that the answer would be the one she sought.

"Ruth."

With an effort, Nancy masked her elation. It would not do to excite Rodney by telling him that she thought she had discovered his long-lost sister. If the evidence which Doctor Stafford could provide should fail to confirm her theory, Rodney would be plunged into deepest despair. Better to keep her suspicions to herself until she had the proof.

"Ruth Brown is a common enough name," she reflected. "For all I know, there may be two Ruths. There isn't much resemblance between the two, either."

As if he had read part of her thoughts, the chauffeur remarked moodily:

"Ruth and I were twins, though not the identical type. Even when we were young, people said we didn't look a great deal alike. Since the war, I've changed so that my best friends wouldn't recognize me."

Nancy arose to leave.

"Rodney, I want you to do me a favor."

"Certainly, Miss Drew."

"Can you come to my house tomorrow afternoon at five o'clock?"

"I think so. Tomorrow is my day off duty."

"Then I'll expect you without fail. Don't forget the hour."

With that Nancy hurried away, leaving the chauffeur to stare after her in bewilderment.

Driving rapidly toward River Heights, she reviewed in her mind the many strange facts she had accumulated. Rodney had a twin sister named Ruth. Reverend Stafford had told her that the twins he had baptized were christened Rodney and Ruth. Now, if the church record would only reveal that the last name was Brown, certain jagged pieces of her jigsaw would fit.

"I'll see the minister the first thing tomorrow," she decided. "I must have all the evidence possible before Ruth and Rodney call at my home."

Nancy did not sleep well that night, for she

was thinking over what might transpire the following day at the appointed hour of five. Immediately after breakfast she called at Reverend Stafford's home. The man conducted her to his study.

"I was hoping that you would drop in today," he said cordially. "At last I have located the record you want."

Nancy's eyes sparkled.

"Reverend Stafford," she said breathlessly, "were the twins you christened named Ruth and Rodney *Brown*?"

The pastor stared incredulously.

"How did you know?"

"I didn't, but now I am convinced I have found the pair whom you baptized so many years ago."

After telling the minister her story Nancy thanked him for his assistance in the case, and left the house in high spirits. A block down the street she heard her name called. Turning around, she saw Bess Marvin waving to her.

"I've been trying to catch you for half a block!" Bess laughed as she came up puffing. "You must be dreaming. I called your name six times."

"I *am* up in the clouds," Nancy admitted. "This is going to be a red letter day in my life. At five o'clock I reunite the separated twins, Rodney and Ruth Brown!"

Such a sweeping statement demanded an explanation, which Nancy was only too glad to give. Bess listened, enthralled.

"Oh, you're a genius!" she praised. "Perhaps you'll soon clear up the parentage of Jay and Janet, too."

"I'm afraid that won't be accomplished so easily."

"You can do anything," Bess maintained staunchly. "Besides, you have a wonderful clue. This is your chance to test it out!"

"What do you mean?"

"Rodney is the father of the babies—I feel convinced of it! After you have reunited him with his sister, he'll feel like a new man. Ask him a few leading questions while he is in the mood to answer."

"It's an embarrassing subject," Nancy smiled.

Bess revealed her annoyance.

"Don't you think he is the father?"

"I'm reserving judgment until after the interview." Nancy glanced down at her wrist watch. "I must run now or I'll be late for luncheon. Tomorrow I'll tell you how everything came out."

CHAPTER XVI

A Happy Reunion

"You're not eating a thing, Nancy."

Anxiously Hannah Gruen hovered near the luncheon table watching her young mistress. Nancy had only toyed with the delicious soufflé which the housekeeper had prepared, and ignored the plate of frosted cakes set before her.

"I'm not hungry, Hannah. I'm so excited about Rodney and Ruth coming!"

"Humph! If it ain't one pair of twins it's another! I declare, no one gives me any consideration in this house. Here I slave all morning baking cake and cooking a fine luncheon. Then your father telephones he won't be home, and you refuse to eat!"

Nancy laughed. "I'll eat the plates if it will please you, Hannah, only I haven't much of an appetite for them now."

"Run along!" The housekeeper grinned in spite of herself. "If you can't eat I guess you can't."

"Your cakes look lovely with the pink and white icing," Nancy praised. "I have an idea! Why not serve them for tea when Ruth and Rodney are here?"

"I might do that," the housekeeper agreed more cheerfully. "I could make hot chocolate, too. Most folks like it better than tea."

Nancy danced from the room into her father's study. There she unlocked a desk drawer and removed the bundle of baby garments and the broken locket. For some time she sat by the window with the articles in her lap, gazing dreamily off into space. If only she could solve the mystery of Jay's and Janet's parentage, how happy she would be!

She tried to read a book, but it was impossible to keep her mind upon the printed page. Time passed slowly. Finally the doorbell rang.

Nancy sprang to her feet, and thrust the bundle of baby clothes into the desk drawer. Before Hannah could reach the front door, Nancy had flung it open to admit Miss Brown.

"I kept my promise, you see," the nurse smiled, following Nancy to the study. "However, I am afraid I must disappoint you."

"You mean you will not accept the position with the Blairs?"

"I have thought it over, but I can't see my way clear to work for such people."

"Then I won't urge you to do so," Nancy said quietly, offering Miss Brown a chair. "I have something here I want to show you."

She took the broken locket from the desk drawer and handed it to the nurse.

"Have you seen this before?"

"Why, yes! It is the one I picked up with the babies!"

"Tell me exactly where you found the locket," Nancy urged. "Was it along the shore?"

"Oh, no. In the boat itself. It was caught in Janet's little dress."

"The locket was broken when you found it?"

"Yes. I don't know what became of the other half."

"And where did you find the boat?"

"It was caught in a clump of logs near shore. It was badly battered—doubtless by the storm. It was leaking. If I hadn't happened along when I did, the babies would have drowned, I'm sure."

"Or else have died of exposure."

"Yes. Jay did catch a terrible cold, but I nursed him through it. Fortunately, both the babies were well bundled up at the time."

"I suppose the old boat was lost," Nancy remarked casually.

"No, I dragged it out of the water. For a long time it was left by the shore. Then an old riverman hauled it away somewhere."

This, Nancy thought, was a point worth noting. If only she could locate the man in question, or examine the boat itself, she might stumble upon an important clue.

"Do you know the man's name?" she asked eagerly.

"Why, yes, I do. It was Enos Crinkle. He has a shack somewhere along the river."

Before Nancy could question the nurse further, the doorbell rang again. She heard Hannah answer it.

The housekeeper had been instructed previously to show any visitors to the study, so Nancy was ready for Rodney when he entered the room. His face showed that he was puzzled at being requested to call at the Drew home.

An awkward moment followed. The man's eyes slowly swept the room, and finally rested upon the nurse. Nancy, with her usual composure, then said:

"You two have met before, I believe."

Recognition flashed over the chauffeur's face as he stared at Ruth Brown.

"Why, you are the agent for baby foods!"

"And you are the Blairs' chauffeur," the nurse returned. "If you have come here to take me to Jolly Folly, you may as well turn around and drive home! I cannot go there!"

Rodney was taken aback at this declaration, for he had not been informed of Nancy's plan to secure a place for the nurse with the Blairs.

"I don't know what you're talking about," Rodney declared.

"You mean Mrs. Blair didn't send you here after me?"

"Certainly not. I came because Miss Drew requested me to do so."

Rodney's eyes moved searchingly to Nancy's face. He seemed to comprehend the situation, for he added quickly:

"Of course, it's none of my affair, but the twins do need a good nurse. If you could be persuaded to come, I'd be only too glad to drive you out as soon as the repairs on my car are finished at the garage."

Nancy could see that Miss Brown was on the verge of refusing a second time. The girl stepped forward, weighing each word lest she spoil everything by saying the wrong thing.

"I have a long story to relate—one which will be of vital interest to both of you. But first let me introduce you. Miss Ruth Brown, may I present Rodney Brown?"

There was a stunned silence as the two stared at each other. The color drained from the chauffeur's face.

"Ruth Brown!" he murmured dazedly. "What a coincidence! I had a twin sister by that name."

"And I had a twin brother named Rodney!" the nurse cried. "There must be some mistake. You aren't my brother, surely?"

"Hear the story I have to tell," Nancy said quietly.

While the two visitors listened breathlessly, she related the absorbing tale of the baptism.

"I remember now that I was christened by a minister named Stafford," Rodney said, staring in awe at the nurse. "My mother often told me so."

"And I still have the baptismal certificate somewhere in my possession!" Ruth added joyfully.

Nancy had never before gazed upon two such radiant faces. Brother and sister were gradually beginning to realize that they had found each other after a long, long separation.

CHAPTER XVII

A HURRY CALL

"THEN you are my long-lost brother! I've searched for you all these years!"

"And to think I didn't recognize my own sister!"

Ruth and Rodney Brown moved forward slowly, as if in a trance. With laughter and tears of joy, they fell into each other's arms.

"Ruth!"

"Rodney!"

Quietly, Nancy stole from the room, softly closing the door behind her. The reunion had been accomplished. Her presence would only detract from the happy scene.

As she stood by the living room window some time later, gazing dreamily out upon the garden, Hannah Gruen came in.

"Is it time to serve my cakes and chocolate yet, Nancy?"

"Oh, dear me, I had forgotten all about it!" Nancy laughed. "Yes, I'm sure this would be an appropriate moment. Ruth and Rodney have had at least half an hour together."

"What are you up to, anyway?" the housekeeper demanded, casting a suspicious glance toward the closed doors of the study. "I don't see why you invite folks here, and then go off and leave them alone."

Nancy laughed heartily.

"I've just reunited a brother and a sister who haven't seen each other in years."

"Oh," Hannah murmured, impressed, "that's different. I'll hurry and put the chocolate on the stove."

While Nancy was debating whether or not to reënter the study, the door opened and Ruth and Rodney emerged, arm in arm. Tears glistened in the nurse's eyes, but her face glowed with happiness.

"Miss Drew, we owe all this to you! How can we ever thank you for what you have done?"

"Please don't try," Nancy said uncomfortably, for praise always embarrassed her. "Reverend Stafford is the one you are indebted to, for without his record the reunion might never have been brought about."

"We'll call on him tomorrow," Rodney promised. "The remainder of this day we must spend together and just reminisce after all these years."

"I had given up all hopes of ever finding my brother," Ruth told Nancy tremulously. "The War Department reported that he had been killed in action. Later this was amended to 'missing in action,' but I never could force myself to believe that he was dead.''

"I had changed so much, I didn't care to have my relatives see me," Rodney explained. "Then, when I had grown less sensitive, I learned that everyone I knew had moved away."

"I traveled about the country, looking for you," said his sister.

"And to think that we should meet at the Blairs' and I failed to recognize you," returned Rodney.

"Everything about me has changed," Ruth admitted ruefully. "I have had so much trouble. Now that we are together again, everything will be all right."

Nancy had not forgotten that Bess wanted her to inquire about Jay and Janet. Adroitly, she led up to the subject.

"I suppose I am deeply interested in them because I am a twin myself," the chauffeur told her. "It made me fairly sick to see Mrs. Blair destroy the only evidence of their parentage."

"But she didn't," Nancy assured him. "I have everything. Mrs. Blair destroyed only some doll clothes which I substituted." This assertion was a great surprise, and the young girl was forced to explain.

"I'm glad of that," Rodney said in relief. "It worried me a lot."

Nancy then told the chauffeur that his sister was the person who had found the babies.

"I've been amply repaid," Ruth declared, "for it is really through the twins that Rodney and I have been reunited."

Nancy at that moment caught a glimpse of Hannah coming from the kitchen with a plate of cakes and a pot of chocolate. She hurried to assist her, when the telephone rang.

"Someone always gets on the wire when I have my hands full!" the housekeeper gasped.

"I'll answer it, Hannah. It's probably Father."

However, the call was not from Carson Drew, but from the Jolly Folly estate. As Nancy took down the receiver, she recognized Colleen's distressed voice.

"Oh, Miss Drew, can you come at once? A terrible thing has happened! The babies have had a bad fall!"

"Are they seriously hurt?" Nancy gasped.

"I think they are dying!"

"Send for the doctor at once!" Nancy ordered tersely. "I'll come as soon as I can."

She wheeled from the phone to face her guests. Ruth already had a suspicion that some disaster had befallen the children.

"Is anything the matter?" she asked tremulously. "The babies aren't sick, are they?"

"They've had a bad fall. I must get a nurse at once."

In this sudden emergency Ruth Brown forgot her firm resolution never to set foot in the Blair home. She gripped Nancy's arm.

"Oh, take me along! I must be with the twins! No one can care for them as well as I!"

Relief flooded over Nancy. In her heart, she had known all the time that the nurse would not fail her.

"My car is at the door!" Nancy cried. "We haven't a second to lose!"

Hannah Gruen, a plate of cakes in one hand, a pot of chocolate in the other, stood aghast.

"You can't go before you've eaten!" she wailed.

"Oh, I'm very sorry, Hannah," Nancy called back over her shoulder. "We're in a big hurry and can't stop for *anything* now!"

Few words were spoken during the swift ride to Jolly Folly. Fear gripped everyone's heart.

"It's all Colleen's fault, I'll wager," the chauffeur muttered once. "She leaves the babies alone half the time."

They drew near the estate. From afar Nancy noticed a car driving hurriedly away.

"Can that be the doctor, I wonder?" she asked her companions.

Rodney fairly snorted.

"Doctor nothing! I've seen that rattle-trap often enough. It belongs to Francis Clancy!"

"Colleen's friend!"

"Yes, he spends hours and hours hanging

around the kitchen. Colleen sneaks off at night with him, too, when she's supposed to be on duty.''

"I'm glad I came," Ruth murmured. "Oh, to think of Jay and Janet being under the care of such a girl! If they die I'll never forgive myself!"

Nancy's face became grim. She, too, felt that she would never forgive herself if any serious harm had befallen the twins. She considered herself to blame for not having reported Colleen's previous carelessness to Mrs. Blair.

She had guessed that the maid was spending too much time with Francis. Now she was convinced that the twins had injured themselves while they had been left alone.

The machine came to a standstill before the Blair residence. Nancy and the Browns flung themselves out of it.

"And the doctor isn't here yet!" Rodney groaned. "Our automobile is the only one parked within the grounds."

"Surely he has had ample time to arrive," Ruth murmured anxiously.

It did not occur to either of them to doubt that Colleen had called the physician, but Nancy began to be suspicious.

Followed closely by Ruth and the chauffeur, the Drew girl ran up the steps to the house. As they jerked open the door, they could hear the heart-rending screams of the infants from the floor above.

"They're in the nursery!" Nancy cried.

"Oh, my poor babies!" Ruth Brown half sobbed.

Fearing the worst, the three rushed blindly for the stairs.

CHAPTER XVIII

COLLEEN'S TREACHERY

COLLEEN, her face white with fear, was pacing the floor, the children in her arms. The more she tried to soothe them, the louder they cried.

Nancy and Ruth Brown, reaching the nursery together, fairly snatched the twins from her. They winced at sight of the infants' swollen and bruised faces. Jay was the more painfully injured; a big bump stood out upon his forehead, and a cut showed above his left eye.

With skillful hands the nurse examined the babies for broken bones. She was relieved to find none. Gradually, as she cuddled the little ones in her arms, their sobs died away.

"Are they seriously hurt?" Nancy questioned anxiously.

"Only bruised severely, I think."

"Where is the doctor?" Nancy inquired, turning to Colleen. "You called him, didn't you?"

Colleen avoided the girl's eyes.

"Well, no, I didn't. You see, I thought if

the doctor came there'd be a bill, and then Mrs. Blair would make a fuss!''

"She'll hear of this anyway,'' Nancy said shortly.

Colleen looked startled.

"I don't believe it will be necessary to call a doctor now,'' Ruth Brown told Nancy, who was hastening toward the telephone. "I'll soon have the babies asleep.''

Colleen relaxed.

"Those awful kids sure get me into lots of trouble.''

"You mean that you get them into plenty!'' Nancy snapped. "Just what happened, Colleen? Tell us everything.''

"Well, to start with, today is Friday, the thirteenth——''

"What has that to do with it?'' Nancy interrupted sternly.

"Things happen on Friday the thirteenth,'' the maid insisted, her eyes wide open. "I told the cook this morning that I just felt the twins were fated——''

"Nonsense!'' Nancy cut in impatiently. "Where were you when the babies fell?''

"I—I——''

Colleen seemed reluctant to answer this question.

"Let me see,'' she hedged. "Why, I was upstairs the same as usual.''

"Weren't you in the garden with Francis?''

Nancy accused. "We saw him driving away as we came up."

Colleen's face flushed.

"Well, come to think of it, I guess I was. He just dropped in for a minute, and I ran down to tell him I couldn't spare a second from the kids!"

"A likely story!" Nancy thought, completely disgusted with the girl.

"Where did you leave the twins while you were gone?" she demanded.

"Right in their cribs. The first thing I knew, I heard a thud and a loud scream. I ran up here and found the babies on the floor. They couldn't have fallen out by themselves! It's supernatural!"

Nancy bent down to examine the cribs. She saw at once that one side dropped down on a hinge. Unquestionably, the careless Colleen had neglected to fasten the lock which held it upright. She pointed this out to the maid.

"I'm sure I fastened the latch," Colleen maintained, though without sufficient conviction. "You won't tell Mrs. Blair, will you? She'll discharge me if she finds out."

"One glance at the babies will convince her that something has happened," Nancy returned. "Colleen, I don't believe you've paid the slightest attention to your duties all day!"

"Oh, I have! Except for just a minute or two—maybe it was five—when I ran down to talk with Francis, I haven't left the nursery!"

Nancy did not believe this story. She rather suspected that Colleen had been arraying herself in Mrs. Blair's fine clothes again, for the girl's face was highly rouged and her own garments gave the appearance of having been donned hastily.

"When did you last give Jay and Janet something to eat?" Ruth Brown questioned, directing a hostile glance toward the maid. "They act hungry to me."

"It couldn't have been more than an hour or so ago."

Rodney had been standing quietly by, marveling at the wonderful way in which his sister and Nancy had taken charge of the babies. Now he stepped forward.

"I'll go down to the kitchen and ask the cook when she last heated their milk."

Colleen shot him a look of hatred.

"Snoop!" she accused.

Rodney paid no attention to her. In a few minutes he returned with the milk and prepared baby food.

"The cook reports that the children haven't had anything to eat all afternoon!"

"Oh, the poor little things!" Ruth exclaimed. "Give me the milk at once, Rodney."

Colleen flashed an angry look at the efficient woman who was usurping her place.

"I don't see what right you have to come

here!" she said disdainfully. "A pedlar woman!"

"How *dare* you call my sister by such a name?" Rodney cried angrily.

Colleen looked dumbfounded.

"Your sister?"

"Yes, my sister. Furthermore, she is a real nurse and knows how to care for babies, which is more than you do!"

"I won't stay here to be insulted!" Colleen said pettishly.

No one protested when she banged out of the nursery. They guessed that she was going to the kitchen to spread the news that Rodney had brought a mysterious sister into the house.

"You shouldn't have spoken so harshly to her," Ruth chided her brother.

"I couldn't help it. She's neglected the babies ever since they have been here. When she talked about you it got the best of me."

Knowing that the twins would now be in safe hands, Nancy decided to take advantage of Colleen's absence to do a little bit of investigating. Quietly she stole into Mrs. Blair's bedroom.

"Just as I thought!" she observed.

Garments were scattered about everywhere. Two elaborate green evening gowns had been dropped carelessly upon the bed. A picture hat lay upon a chair. Shoes were strewn over the floor.

"Colleen has been dressing up again," Nancy

thought grimly. "I might have known she'd never keep her promise to me."

Nancy was by nature orderly in her habits. She began to pick up the clothes, returning them to the hooks in the closet. When she realized what she was doing, she laughed shortly.

"Here I go, helping that girl again when I should really tell Mrs. Blair about her. Oh, well, there will be trouble enough when she sees Jay and Janet. I may as well finish this job."

After putting things in order she returned to the nursery where she found Colleen. The girl eyed her suspiciously.

"Didn't I hear you walking around in Mrs. Blair's bedroom?" she asked maliciously.

"If you did, you may be sure I wasn't trying on any of her gowns!" Nancy retorted pointedly.

Colleen pretended not to understand. But when Nancy's back was turned, the nursemaid glared upon her bitterly.

"I'll fix her for spying!" she thought. "She can't take away my job and not pay for it!"

Nancy had no intention of taking away the girl's position. In talking with Mrs. Blair about a new nurse, she had thoughtfully suggested that Ruth Brown be engaged in addition to Colleen. That the two could never work together was evident, however.

Unaware that Colleen was plotting to involve

her in trouble, Nancy chatted pleasantly with Miss Brown.

"I never saw anyone so skillful at handling babies as you are," she praised. "If you were to stay here, I'd feel that the children would be in safe hands."

"I've been thinking the matter over," the nurse said slowly. "Perhaps I might consider coming after all."

"Oh, I wish you would!"

"My brother works here and I should like to be near him. Since I have seen the twins, I can't bear to leave them again. They have lost too much weight since they were taken from the Home."

"If you'll promise to accept the position, I am sure I can arrange matters satisfactorily with the Blairs," Nancy eagerly assured Ruth Brown.

The two had forgotten Colleen completely. But the malicious girl was taking in every word of their conversation.

"So she thinks Miss Brown will get my job, does she?" the girl said sneeringly to herself. "We'll see about that!"

Colleen slipped quietly from the room. Her absence passed unnoticed.

A few minutes later the front doorbell rang several times. It was not answered. Then the ringing began again.

"The servants never seem to be of much use

in this house," Nancy remarked to Miss Brown. "I'll see who it is."

The staccato of the bell told her that the caller was becoming very impatient. Nancy quickened her steps. Flinging open the door, she stood face to face with Edwin McNeery. He doffed his hat politely.

"The Blairs in?"

"Not yet," Nancy told him. "I'm expecting them at any moment. Would you care to wait?"

The producer passed before her into the library.

"Will I wait?" he laughed unpleasantly. "That's all I ever do. The Blairs were supposed to be at rehearsal at three today and they didn't show up!"

"Then I presume they signed the contract," Nancy said, for she had not heard of their action in the matter.

"Sure they signed it! I knew they would."

"What decision did you reach regarding the babies?" Nancy asked mischievously.

"We're letting the matter hang fire for a few days," McNeery admitted reluctantly. "I don't care if the Blairs keep their brats, so long as they don't let them interfere with our business."

Nancy concealed a smile. She inferred that the signing of the contract had ended in a draw. McNeery had won his point about the salary; Kitty Blair had won hers regarding the babies.

"If rehearsals don't go off any better than they did today, my revue will be a flop!" the producer told her, biting savagely at a cigar. "Where did they go today?"

"I'm sure I don't know," Nancy returned. She moved to the window. "A car is coming now. I think it must be the Blairs."

Her guess was correct. The actor and actress came storming into the house, quarreling about some trivial matter. Finding McNeery in the library, they instantly quieted down.

The producer did not mince words.

"Where were you this afternoon?" he fairly shouted. "Why weren't you at rehearsal?"

Kitty struck a haughty pose.

"How dare you speak to me in such a tone? I'll attend rehearsals when I choose."

"Then you'll break your contract! I've had just about enough of your temperament and your babies! Either you attend to business after this or you quit! Get me?"

The argument went on. Nancy was forced to listen, for Kitty stood with her back to the door. The girl could not leave the room without asking the actress to move.

The commotion carried to the floor above. Colleen stole down the stairs to learn what was going on. Unknown to those in the library, she stood in the living room, quietly listening.

Her eye suddenly fell upon Mrs. Blair's pocketbook which had carelessly been dropped upon the table. With a low cry Colleen snatched it up and opened it, unobserved by anyone.

She drew from it the actress's diamond locket and chain. For a moment the malicious girl held the jewelry in her hand as if reluctant to part with it. Then, with a triumphant chuckle, she ran out to the place where Nancy's car was parked. Hastily she looked about her to see if anyone was within sight. The coast was clear.

"I guess *this* will fix Nancy Drew!" she chortled wickedly.

Deliberately she dropped the valuable diamond locket into the side pocket of the Drew girl's machine.

CHAPTER XIX

A New Clue

EDWIN McNEERY and the Blairs meanwhile continued their argument in the library.

"We must come to some agreement," the producer insisted. "Either you attend rehearsals after this, or the show doesn't go on. Which shall it be?"

"I can't see any sense in making such a fuss over nothing," Kitty said petulantly, "but if it will satisfy you, then we'll attend all your old rehearsals!"

Aloofly, Kitty and Johnny stood aside to permit the man to leave. They closed the library door after him, shutting themselves in for a private conference.

"They're the limit!" McNeery laughed ruefully to Nancy. "If all my actors and actresses were like them, I'd commit suicide!"

Nancy could not help smiling to herself.

"My wife was a real actress," McNeery continued in a confidential tone. "You may have heard of her—Sylvia McNeery."

Nancy listened attentively.

"She had a fine career ahead of her," the producer went on reminiscently. "But Sylvia was peculiar. She preferred a home life to a career on the stage. We argued about it a lot and finally she left me.''

''That's too bad,'' Nancy returned sympathetically.

Secretly she was of the opinion that Sylvia McNeery had done the sensible thing by leaving the producer. However, his voice seemed less harsh when he spoke of his wife, and Nancy surmised that he had taken the blow of her leaving much to heart.

''I'd give a good deal if I could locate her,'' McNeery declared. ''I guess I didn't think much about her until she was gone.''

Impulsively he opened his wallet and removed a small snapshot which he handed to Nancy.

''That's a picture of my wife,'' he said proudly.

Nancy stared down at the sweet, intelligent face of a beautiful woman.

''She's very lovely.''

''Yes, she was good looking all right. And she could act, too! Her name would be in electric lights today if she hadn't been carried away by a lot of silly notions!''

The producer returned the photograph to his wallet, and hastily said good-bye. Nancy watched him jump into his car and drive away.

Hearing the door slam, Mr. and Mrs. Blair emerged from the library.

"I'm glad that pest is gone!" Kitty exclaimed. "He drives me wild with his stupid demands."

"Let's go upstairs and have a look at the twins," Johnny proposed. "I just thought of a new acrobatic stunt I must teach Jay!"

Nancy knew that another scene would soon take place. Reluctantly she followed the Blairs upstairs to the nursery.

Kitty took one look at the bruised faces of the babies and wheeled wrathfully upon Colleen.

"What have you been doing to them?"

"Not a thing," the servant maintained, beginning to sob. "They fell out of their cribs."

"I'll bet you dropped them!"

"I didn't, I tell you! I get blamed for everything!"

At this point Nancy intervened. She quietly explained what had happened, then introduced Ruth Brown to them.

"This is the nurse I was telling you about, Mrs. Blair. I brought her with me today."

"She seems to know a lot about babies," the actress observed, quieting down somewhat. "If she can keep them from crying, and not be dropping them all the time, I can expect no more."

"I can do far more than that, I know," Miss Brown said with a smile.

"Stay here tonight," the actress directed.

"If you get along well with the babies, we'll talk about the position tomorrow."

"I've taken the best care of the kids that anyone could," Colleen whined. "I've fetched and carried for them and scarcely left them an instant. It wasn't my fault that they had to fall out of bed!"

"You've been careless from the day I hired you! You drop bottles—that is bad enough, and allow the infants to fall from their cribs. You spend all your time holding hands in the garden with that boy friend of yours!"

Colleen hung her head, meanwhile regarding Nancy balefully from the corner of her eye. She felt that the River Heights girl was the cause of the severe reprimand she was receiving.

"At least, I've fixed her!" she thought vindictively. "If I lose my job she'll pay for it!"

Mrs. Blair continued her tirade, working herself into a frenzy of rage. Nancy began to feel sorry for Colleen, and succeeded in soothing the actress by attracting her attention to Miss Brown.

"It was good of you to come out this afternoon," Mrs. Blair said in a calmer voice. "Have you had much experience caring for babies?"

"Why, yes," Ruth Brown responded. "I spent several months at the Home in addition to my regular training."

"The Home?" Mrs. Blair inquired, her penciled eyebrows raised quizzically.

Nancy shot a warning glance at the nurse. It would never do to let Mrs. Blair know that the nurse had come from the Selkirk Home, for the actress did not want to be reminded of the twins' past.

Ruth Brown was quick to comprehend.

"A home for babies some distance from here."

"Oh, I see. It happens that my own twins come from a Foundling Home, though I intend that they shall never know of it. If you become their nurse, I hope you'll grow fond of them."

Miss Brown turned her face toward the children.

"I am sure that I shall grow more and more fond of them."

It was getting late, and Nancy announced that she must hasten home. Mrs. Blair thanked her dramatically and profusely for her kindness in coming to the house. Before leaving, Nancy managed to have a word alone with Ruth Brown.

"I feel sure you will get the position now."

"If I don't do something to offend Mrs. Blair in the meantime! She has such a harsh tongue. However, I'll put up with it. Anything to be near the babies."

As the girl was leaving, Miss Brown could not keep from issuing a word of warning.

"I believe Colleen means to make trouble for you, Miss Drew. I couldn't help but notice how she glared at you while Mrs. Blair was scolding her."

Nancy laughed lightly.

"Oh, she can't harm me, for I have no position to lose. You are the one to be on guard. Colleen is jealous because you are taking her place."

Nancy dismissed the nursemaid from her mind as she sprang into her car and drove rapidly toward River Heights. She did not dream that in the side pocket of the automobile she was carrying a valuable diamond locket which was to involve her in serious trouble before very long.

Nancy and her father were at breakfast the next morning when Hannah came in to say that Rodney Brown was at the door.

"Ask him to come in," Mr. Drew directed.

"I did, but he refused. He said he had a message for Miss Nancy."

The girl arose.

"It's probably about the babies, Father. I'll see what he wants."

Rodney was waiting on the veranda, hat in hand. He smiled as Nancy greeted him cordially.

"Won't you come in?"

"I can't stop. I'm supposed to be on duty now at Jolly Folly. The Blairs sleep late,

though, so I thought I'd have time to bring you
a bit of news.''

''The twins aren't worse, are they?''

''No, Ruth said they were much better this
morning.''

''I'm glad to hear that. What is it you have
to tell me?''

''Colleen has been discharged!''

''Really!''

''After you left late yesterday she had another fuss with Mrs. Blair. They told her to
pack up and leave!''

''I see,'' said Nancy thoughtfully. ''And is
your sister to have full charge of the twins?''

''Yes, Mrs. Blair was happy to have her
stay. If Ruth and I could only take the children with us we'd like to find a new place to
work.''

''Of course that's impossible—at least for
the time being.''

''I suppose so,'' Rodney sighed. ''Everything about the babies is in such an upheaval.
You know, it was sort of queer—Ruth finding
them, and all.''

''Yes, it was,'' Nancy agreed.

The chauffeur was turning to leave when he
thought of something else he wanted to say.

''Colleen was talking a good bit in the
kitchen this morning. She was blaming you
for her being discharged.''

''I expected that.''

"Well, I just thought I'd tell you. When she dislikes anyone she sometimes stoops to some mighty underhanded tricks."

"I'll probably never see her again," Nancy said, smiling. "Thank you for warning me, though."

The girl returned to the breakfast table. She reported the conversation to her father, omitting the warning Rodney had given her.

"You know, talking with him reminded me of something I nearly forgot!" she declared enthusiastically a few moments later. "Yesterday Miss Brown told me that a man named Enos Crinkle has in his possession the old boat in which the twins were found!"

"That's interesting. But just how will it aid you in learning the identity of the babies?"

"I have a hunch that the craft may yield up some clue."

"It's probably rotted away by this time."

"The boat or the clue?" Nancy laughed.

"Both."

"The clue I'm looking for can't deteriorate. It may seem like a wild chase on my part, but just the same I'm going to trace down this man Crinkle!"

Carson Drew had learned of the amazing manner in which his daughter had reunited the Brown twins. He accordingly intimated that Nancy should feel satisfied with such a splendid piece of detective work.

"I'll not rest until I've located the parents of Jay and Janet!" Nancy announced with determination. "Bringing Ruth and Rodney together was just a side issue of the main case."

"I admire your pluck in sticking to it all," her father said proudly. "I hope you wade through it, too. But if a skiff is your only remaining clue, I'm afraid you will be doomed to disappointment."

"Wait and see!" Nancy laughed confidently.

She hurried away to telephone her chums, Bess and George, and asked if they wanted to go with her to find the old boat. They were eager for the adventure, and proposed that they bring a picnic lunch with them. Nancy hurried to the kitchen to ask Hannah to pack a box of food for her.

"Now you'll be gone again all day, and my nice cakes never will be eaten!" the housekeeper complained.

"Put them in the lunch basket—every single one!" Nancy pleaded. "Bess, George and I can easily eat a dozen."

Hannah brightened and went cheerfully about the task of preparing the lunch. Nancy went up to her room to dress for the outing.

"I'll locate Enos Crinkle if he lives along the river," she told herself determinedly. "And what's more, if I find that old boat, I'll make it give up its clue!"

CHAPTER XX

ENOS CRINKLE'S BOAT

TEN o'clock found Nancy, Bess and George driving through the outskirts of Selkirk. As they came within view of the Foundling Home, Nancy proposed that they stop to inquire if anyone knew the way to Enos Crinkle's shack.

She left her chums sitting in the car and entered the building alone. Mrs. Roberts, the matron, chanced to be in the entrance hall at the time, and recognized the River Heights girl at once.

"Did you locate the record you were looking for the other day, Miss Drew?" she asked kindly.

"Yes. But I was sorry I couldn't talk with you longer when I was here."

"I guess we were both in a hurry. Oh, by the way, we have a new nurse to take the place of Miss Brown who left us."

"You may be interested to know that Miss Brown is now employed by the Blairs," Nancy informed her in turn.

"I am very glad to hear that," the matron beamed. "She will make them a splendid

170

nurse. And it will mean so much to her to be near the babies she loves.''

The matron was a very busy person; therefore, Nancy did not want to take up too much of her time. She hurriedly explained the mission that had brought her to Selkirk.

''Enos Crinkle's shack is about a mile down the river,'' Mrs. Roberts directed her. ''You'll find it set back from the bank a little way, in a dense wood. I believe you can drive within a few yards of the place.''

Nancy thanked her and returned to her waiting friends. They followed the winding river road, and when the speedometer registered exactly a mile, came to the end of it.

''I guess we shall have to walk from here,'' Nancy announced.

Bess carefully removed the lunch basket from the rumble-seat.

''I'm not going to leave the food here,'' she declared. ''Someone very hungry might come along and find it too tempting to resist.''

A short hike brought the girls within view of a tumble-down cabin. The place looked deserted at first glance, but Nancy saw a thin curl of smoke swirling up from the chimney. She went to the door and knocked.

''Come in!'' a voice bellowed.

For a moment the girls were hesitant about obeying. They waited, and the door was flung open. A short, stocky man with loose-fitting clothes and a corncob pipe in his mouth peered out at them. His face wrinkled into a smile as he saw the girls.

"Well, shiver my timbers if it ain't three gals!" Then he noticed the lunch basket which Bess carried. "Sure, I know you've come to ask if you can use my picnic grounds."

"And may we?" Nancy inquired, smiling.

"Go right ahead. Most folks don't even bother to ask. Just clean the leavin's after you're through, that's all I ask."

"Have you by any chance a boat for rent?" Nancy next questioned the man, deciding to lead up to her objective gradually.

"I have one of my own," the riverman told her, "but I don't let it out much."

"You haven't an old one?"

"The wreck of a skiff I found near Selkirk is lying on the beach by the picnic grounds. But don't make the mistake of trying to float that old tub!"

"Was that the rowboat in which some twin babies were found?" Nancy asked eagerly.

The riverman stared in surprise.

"Yes, that's the one."

"May we take a look at it?"

"I suppose you can, but there isn't much to see. It's fallen all to pieces. I've been intendin' to chop it up for kindlin' wood, but never got around to it. Wait a moment and I'll show you where it is."

Nancy caught a glimpse of the wrecked craft lying half buried in sand. With a cry of joy she ran toward it.

"Can't see anything to get so excited about in an old tub like that," Enos Crinkle chuckled. "Wait until I show you my boat! Just painted her a week ago, and she's a beauty."

By this time the party had reached the derelict. The girls could not help but laugh at the hopeless way in which Nancy regarded the wreckage.

Very little remained of the boat. Several of the decayed timbers had fallen away, the oars were gone, and the stern had been bashed in. It rested bottom side up in the sand.

"May we turn it over, Mr. Crinkle?" Nancy queried.

"Oh, Nancy, why bother with the old thing?" Bess cut in. "Surely you don't expect to find any clues after all these months!"

"If there ever were any, they'd have vanished long before this," George added.

Nancy refused to let her friends discourage her. She turned to the riverman.

"Will you help me lift the boat?" she asked.

Obligingly he gripped the battered stern, and together they turned over the skiff.

"You see!" Bess exclaimed, almost triumphantly. "There's nothing there!"

Nancy did not answer. She leaned over and removed the slats in the bottom of the boat. In their half-decayed state they ripped out easily.

"I don't see what you're looking for," George said in bewilderment.

"I've found it!" Nancy exclaimed suddenly.

She reached down and caught up a tiny object which had lain half hidden beneath the slat. It was a dirty bit of metal—the missing half of the heart-shaped locket!

"Well, of all things!" Bess ejaculated.

"Nancy, you're a wonder for locating things in the most obscure places!" George marveled.

"That trinket must have been in the boat when I hauled it up here on shore," Enos Crinkle said, scratching his head in bewilderment. "What is it, anyhow?"

"The missing half of a locket," Nancy explained excitedly. "Oh, I was sure I'd find it here!"

"Now that you have it, I can't see what good it will do," Bess declared. "We're no nearer a solution to the mystery than we were before."

Nancy had her own opinion about the matter. With a piece of cloth which she found on the ground, she began to polish the broken locket. Bess and George came over to see what she was doing.

"Why, I believe I see an initial!" George cried.

"Three of them," Nancy corrected quietly. "Can you make them out?"

"The first is S!" Bess deciphered.

"And the second is M!" George said in awe.

"S. M. N." Nancy read aloud. "Now for whom could those letters stand?"

"Perhaps the mother's name," George suggested. "Oh, Nancy, I believe you've stumbled upon a real clue as to the parentage of the babies."

"She didn't exactly stumble," Bess corrected with a laugh. "She reasoned it all out—and we tried to discourage her, too."

"Even Father thought I was starting on a wild chase," Nancy declared. "Now, if I can find a woman who has these initials!"

Enos Crinkle had been listening intently to the conversation.

"If you're looking for the parents of those babies maybe I can give you a tip!" he offered.

Nancy could have hugged the old riverman, so happy was she at his words.

"What do you know about them?" she demanded eagerly.

"I don't know anything about the parents," Enos Crinkle admitted, "but I did find something in the bottom of the boat when I dragged it out of the water."

"What?" the girls queried breathlessly.

"An old newspaper."

The faces of both George and Bess fell at these words, but Nancy grew even more excited.

"Have you that paper now, Mr. Crinkle?"

"No, it was soaking wet, so I threw it away."

"You didn't notice which one it was, did you?"

"Yes, the *Crown Point Star.*"

"Why, Crown Point is only about thirty miles from River Heights!" Bess exclaimed.

"Girls, this may turn out to be the best clue we've discovered yet," Nancy cried. "Crown Point is situated on this same river, too! Mr. Crinkle, I don't suppose you noticed the date of that newspaper by any chance, did you?"

"Well, I did at the time. Seems to me it was September the 13th."

Nancy made a mental note of the date.

"Girls, we must go to Crown Point at once and see if we can trace the twins' parents!" she exclaimed. "What could be more logical than that they came either from that place, or else passed through it?"

"How shall we go about finding them if they are there?" Bess asked, perplexed. "Go from house to house ringing doorbells?"

"I doubt if we'd gain anything by using such a method. If the parents were well known in Crown Point, more than likely someone would have traced their relationship to the twins long ago."

"Then I don't see how we can make any progress," George said flatly.

Nancy dangled the missing half of the locket before her chum's eyes.

"See these initials? Someone at Crown Point may recognize them! And we have the newspaper date to help us, too!"

Gradually Bess and George grew enthusiastic over the proposed trip.

"Let's start this minute!" Nancy pleaded.

"Not until we've eaten our picnic lunch," Bess responded firmly. "I've brought it all the way from the car, and I don't want to carry it back again."

"You'll find a nice picnic ground over yonder," Enos Crinkle said, pointing toward a grove which overlooked the winding river. "I put in a pump last year so you can have all the fresh water you want."

Nancy did not care to stop to eat at such an exciting time, but George and Bess were firm on this point. Laughingly she gave in. Then, thanking the old riverman for his kindness, they carried the lunch basket to the place indicated.

The girls spread the cloth upon one of the tables and arranged the delicious food they had brought from home. Bess and George had excellent appetites after their long ride. Presently they noticed that Nancy was scarcely touching her food.

"Don't mind me, girls," she apologized. "I guess I can't eat just now. I'm too thrilled over our discoveries today!"

"I thought by this time you were a cold-blooded detective who never became excited over anything,'' Bess laughed.

"I wish that were true, but it isn't. I'm all a-tremble at the hope of finding the twins' parents. I just feel that something will develop at Crown Point!''

While Bess and George hurriedly finished eating, Nancy withdrew the missing half of the locket from her pocket and examined it again. Presently she put it away and glanced out across the river.

"Girls!'' she exclaimed. "A boat is landing at the beach! Tell me, am I seeing things, or is that Colleen?''

"Why, it is!'' George cried in amazement. "And that red-haired friend of hers, too! What brought them here?''

"Just out for a boat ride, I imagine,'' Nancy returned. "I suppose Colleen has plenty of time on her hands, now that she has lost her job. I hope she doesn't blame me too much.''

Hurriedly the girls began to gather up their things, for they had no desire to meet Colleen or Francis. They saw the two beach their boat and unload a lunch hamper.

Unaware that other picnickers were upon the grounds already, Colleen and Francis placed their basket upon a nearby table. A growth of high bushes cut off their view of Nancy and her friends.

The girls could hear the two talking earnestly, and from Colleen's tone they knew that she was displeased about something. It was impossible for them to avoid hearing what she was saying, for the wind was in their direction. Nancy paid no heed until her own name was spoken.

"Nancy Drew will wish she never had had me fired!" the girl said bitterly to her companion.

"The cat!" George murmured under her breath. "I'm going around there and tell her a thing or two!"

Nancy placed a restraining hand upon her chum's shoulder.

"Wait!"

Colleen's voice had grown louder. As the girls listened, they distinctly heard her say:

"I guess I fixed Nancy Drew all right! The police will have her in their clutches within forty-eight hours!"

CHAPTER XXI

BEHIND THE CURTAIN

NANCY and her chums had no intentions of leaving the scene. Convinced that Colleen and Francis were engaged in some sinister plot, they cautiously crept closer.

In her anxiety to hear them, George moved far out on a little promontory overlooking the river, which provided a clear view of the picnic spot where Colleen and Francis had spread their lunch.

"Do come back," Nancy whispered anxiously. "The bank may cave in at any——"

The warning died in her throat. George let out a wild yell as the river bank suddenly gave way beneath her. To the horror of her friends, she toppled forward, falling with a great splash into the water a few feet below!

"She'll drown!" Bess cried fearfully.

Nancy already was plunging down the bank. She found George sitting upright in two feet of water, her face and hands covered with mud.

"Look at me!" the girl moaned.

Nancy waded out and helped her to her feet. "Are you hurt?"

Gingerly George moved her arms and legs.

"Everything seems to work all right," she said ruefully. "But look at my clothes!"

"They could stand a trip to the cleaner's," Nancy admitted, laughing.

The girls had forgotten Colleen and Francis completely. The appearance of the two from behind the bushes, however, reminded them that they were in an awkward position.

"Spying, weren't you!" Colleen said accusingly, before anyone could speak. "Trying to hear what we said!"

"Have you a guilty conscience?" Nancy asked sharply.

"Of course I haven't! And *I* don't go prying and snooping around!"

"You followed us here from River Heights!" Francis berated, regarding Nancy with antagonism.

"We were picnicking on these grounds long before you came," Nancy retorted coldly. "However, I am not ashamed to admit that I was interested in your conversation, for I heard my name mentioned."

Francis and Colleen exchanged frightened glances. How much had Nancy heard?

"Let's get away from here," Colleen said quickly to her companion. "We can find some other place where folks won't be eavesdropping!"

They quickly gathered up their things,

launched their boat, and rowed rapidly downstream.

"Good riddance!" Bess remarked feelingly. "Nancy, what do you think they were plotting to do?"

"I'm sure I don't know. If George hadn't tumbled into the river we might have found out what they were up to."

"I'm terribly sorry," George murmured contritely. "I hope you don't think I did it on purpose!"

"Hardly," Nancy laughed. "We must get you home as soon as we can."

"And give up your trip to Crown Point? You were counting on it, Nancy."

"It can wait until another day."

"You're disappointed, I know. Why do I have to be so awkward, anyway?"

Nancy and Bess led the dejected girl back to the parked automobile. She insisted upon sitting in the rumble-seat so that she would not plaster the upholstery with mud.

It was growing late when the girls reached their respective homes. Hannah met Nancy at the door of the Drew residence.

"You had a telephone call this afternoon from Jolly Folly."

"Anything important, Hannah?"

"It was from Mrs. Blair. She seemed excited about something."

"She always is," Nancy remarked wearily.

"She said to tell you to drive out just as soon as you got home. And to bring your father, too."

"What does she want with him?" Nancy asked alertly.

"She wouldn't say."

"I can't imagine any legal matters that would require his services," Nancy mused thoughtfully. "It seems strange, asking both of us to come. Has Father arrived yet?"

There was no need to answer, for at that moment Carson Drew drove into the garage. Nancy went out to deliver the message.

"The last place in the world that I care to visit is Jolly Folly!" he announced firmly. "I'm not going!"

"Oh, you must!" Nancy pleaded. "It may be something important."

"Just a whim of that silly actress, more than likely," Mr. Drew growled. "I have a book I want to read."

"Let it go for tonight," Nancy wheedled. "You know you don't like to have me drive alone over dark roads."

"Well, if you're determined to go, I suppose I can stand it. But we'll make the visit short and snappy!"

The attorney would not think of starting for the Blair estate without having had his dinner. Nancy went to the kitchen to urge Hannah to prepare it as quickly as possible.

"How were the cakes?" the housekeeper asked casually as she dished up some mashed potatoes.

"The cakes?" With a guilty start, Nancy recalled that the picnic had ended before anyone had touched them. She stammered:

"I'm sure they were as delicious as they looked!" Then she ran from the kitchen before the housekeeper could ask her any more questions.

Eight o'clock found Carson Drew and his daughter at the Blair estate. A maid answered the bell and conducted them to the living room where the actor and actress awaited them.

Mrs. Blair arose to greet them, but there was a certain restraint in her manner which Nancy noticed at once. She did not have long to wonder what might be wrong.

"I think I have been robbed!" Mrs. Blair announced dramatically.

"Robbed!" Nancy echoed. "Are you sure?"

"My diamond locket has mysteriously disappeared. I've searched the house from top to bottom and can't find it."

"Did you value it highly?" Mr. Drew inquired.

"It was worth at least eight thousand dollars, and I carried no insurance on it."

"Have you notified the police?" Nancy questioned.

"No, I didn't think it was a case for them to

handle. I thought you might be able to tell me what became of the locket, Miss Drew!''

"I?" Nancy repeated. "I don't know what it looks like!"

She was conscious of the sharp glance which Mrs. Blair bestowed upon her. Carson Drew also observed the expression, and his lips tightened into a thin line.

"Colleen told me before she left that you had telephoned to someone about a locket."

Nancy rapidly reviewed the various telephone calls she had made while at Jolly Folly. She could not recall having mentioned a locket —even the broken one she had found—to anyone. Moreover, Colleen certainly had not heard Nancy's telephone call to Hannah the day the twins had been adopted. With a sinking heart it dawned upon her that Colleen had involved her in a plot.

"She must have been mistaken, Mrs. Blair."

"Another thing, Miss Drew. My friend, Boots Dunbar, reported that she had seen you in the garden one evening with something that shone like gold in your hand. You hurried away before she could question you."

"Are you sure that you had lost your locket at that time?" Nancy asked adroitly.

Mrs. Blair was momentarily nonplussed.

"I don't know when I lost it," she confessed. "I had it in my pocketbook, and when I went to get it this afternoon it was gone."

"It seems to me you were unwise to keep a valuable piece of jewelry in such a place," Mr. Drew interposed.

"That's neither here nor there," the actress said impatiently. "My locket is gone and I mean to get it back!"

"But why question Nancy? I am sure she knows nothing of it."

"Perhaps she does, and perhaps she doesn't," the actress responded tartly. "Let me ask you one thing, Miss Drew. Weren't you in my bedroom while I was gone?"

Nancy felt herself fairly trapped.

"Yes, I went there to take back a gown that Colleen had worn while you were away. She ripped it in trying it on and I mended it for her."

Mrs. Blair accepted this excuse in stony silence. Although she was careful to make no accusations, it was plain to both Nancy and her father that the actress did not believe a word of what the girl had said.

"I assure you that the only reason I went to your room was because I was trying to shield Colleen," Nancy continued earnestly. "If you will look at the drape of your red evening gown——"

She broke off suddenly, her eyes riveted upon the heavy velvet curtains directly behind Mrs. Blair. Distinctly she had seen them move!

CHAPTER XXII

AN ACCUSATION

IN A flash Nancy had crossed the room and flung apart the velvet curtains. A cringing man stood revealed.

Carson Drew sprang to his feet with a low exclamation of anger. He recognized Abe Jacobs, an unscrupulous lawyer who long had made a living by questionable means. The two men were enemies.

"Are you sure you haven't a few dictaphones concealed around the room also, Mrs. Blair?" the River Heights attorney inquired sarcastically. "Really, this is going a bit too far!"

"I have a right to employ a detective if I choose!" the actress said with a toss of her head.

"Are you aware of this man's reputation?" Mr. Drew demanded.

"Certainly I am. He always wins his cases."

Carson Drew smiled grimly, for he recalled a great many that Abe Jacobs had not won— cases in which the two men had engaged in a bitter fight over moral as well as legal rights.

"I have reason to question your daughter," Mrs. Blair went on heatedly. "She thought she was pulling the wool over my eyes, but I knew what was going on all the time!"

"What *are* you talking about?" Nancy asked impatiently.

"I'm talking about the way you go around trying to find the mother of the twins! Colleen told me everything."

Nancy did not attempt to refute the charge. Mrs. Blair continued angrily:

"You're trying to ruin my career, that's what you are up to! If you find their mother I'll have no end of bad luck."

"How ridiculous! As if that could bring you bad luck!" Nancy scoffed.

"I've gone by signs all my life, haven't I, Johnny? If the mother or father of those babies comes back to claim them, my new show will be a failure!"

Nancy and her father were completely disgusted at such superstitious beliefs, but they realized it would be useless for them to try to reason with the Blairs. Mr. Drew turned his attention once more to the smirking Abe Jacobs.

"I don't know how much you have heard behind those curtains," he said curtly, "but I'm giving you fair warning. Print a word of what was said here tonight and you'll have me to reckon with!"

"Perhaps you'll be easier to handle this time," the lawyer leered. "No doubt your daughter's reputation is of vital concern to you, Mr. Drew!"

Carson Drew restrained himself with an effort. His face flushed angrily but his voice was composed.

"You've had your warning, Jacobs. Print one accusation against my daughter and I'll sue you for slander!"

Picking up his hat and cane, Mr. Drew conducted Nancy from the house. As they were stepping into the car a woman came running across the lawn toward them. It was Ruth Brown.

"I couldn't help hearing part of what that dreadful woman said!" she exclaimed in distress. "I want you to know I don't believe a word of it."

"Thank you," Nancy said gratefully. "I'm not much concerned with her silly accusations. I'm more interested in finding the mother of the twins—even if it should ruin the Blairs' show!"

"Oh, I wish you could! The Blairs aren't fit to have children. Even a mother without a penny of money could rear them better than they do. Love is what they need."

"And perhaps they shall have it," Nancy told her. "I think I have a real clue at last!"

"I'm so glad! Even if it means giving up

the babies myself—and that will be hard—I hope you locate the true parents."

Miss Brown hurried back into the house, fearful lest she be seen. During the ride home Nancy and her father had little to say to each other. They realized they were faced with an awkward situation. Abe Jacobs had gained Mrs. Blair's confidence, and the unscrupulous man would overlook no opportunity to embarrass Mr. Drew. He could strike best by involving Nancy in some kind of trouble.

"Don't you worry about this affair," the attorney said kindly, reaching over to squeeze her hand. "I know how to handle men of the Jacobs stamp."

"I'm sorry to have involved you, Father. I didn't realize anything like this could happen when I set out to solve the parentage of Jay and Janet."

"Don't give it a thought," Mr. Drew said carelessly. "You just go right ahead and find the babies' mother and father if you can."

"You're a peach, Father! I knew you'd stand by me."

Nancy went cheerfully to bed a little later. After she had retired, Carson Drew sat thoughtfully at his desk. Abe Jacobs had him in a bad spot.

"It will be a bitter fight," he reflected. "And that man will stoop to anything. But I'll spend a fortune before I'll see him hurt

Nancy's reputation!" His eyes looked worried.

Mr. Drew was up early the next morning. When Nancy came down to breakfast, she saw that he had bought three papers, which were spread out before him.

"Did they dare print the story?" she demanded apprehensively.

"I don't want you to read the papers, Nancy. It will only upset you."

She took them before her father could prevent her.

"No. I insist upon knowing the worst. Oh! This is Jacobs's work."

"The articles are very cleverly worded. While he doesn't actually say you took the locket, he causes the reader to infer it."

"This is dreadful!" Nancy cried.

"Ridiculous! Nearly everyone here knows Abe Jacobs is a crook. Then, too, your side of the story shall appear in the evening paper. I'll write it myself."

Nancy brightened somewhat. Then she grew depressed again as she skimmed over the defaming stories.

"Furthermore, I am instituting slander suits at once against the Blairs, Abe Jacobs, and the newspapers that printed the stories. If the papers retract I may drop the suits later."

"It surely means a great deal to have a lawyer in the family at a time like this," Nancy remarked. "I guess I'll trust my future to you and run off to Crown Point today. I can't bear the thought of answering a lot of foolish questions."

"An excellent idea," her father said approvingly. "The reporters will be after you like flies."

Even as he spoke, the doorbell rang. Hannah entered the breakfast room to report that a newspaperman wanted to talk to Nancy.

"I'll not speak to him," the girl said.

"Slip out the back way, Nancy," her father advised. "I'll handle this gentleman."

While Mr. Drew conducted the reporter to his study, his daughter quietly stole to the garage. A minute later she was speeding swiftly down the street.

"I may as well go to Crown Point!" she decided. "If I stay in River Heights I'll have no peace at all."

She heard her name called and slammed on the brakes. It was too late now to pretend she had not recognized the man, for Edwin McNeery came running over to the car.

"I just saw the story about Kitty Blair's stolen locket in the morning paper!" he shouted.

Nancy bit her lip in annoyance. The man was worse than a town crier!

"I believe you are more upset over it than I am, Mr. McNeery," she said, forcing a smile.

"It's going to cost me money."

"I wish you would explain yourself. How does it involve you?"

"Plenty. You are mighty popular around this part of the country."

"I have a number of friends."

"Your father is influential, too. Now, I've been in the show business a good many years, and I've learned that you can't depend on the public for much of anything. Take this story about the diamond locket, for instance. Folks may be contrary enough to turn against the Blairs instead of you!"

"I really don't see what you are getting at," Nancy said in annoyance.

"Just this." McNeery pounded his fist against the car door for emphasis. "If the public turns against the Blairs, my show will be ruined."

"I'm sorry if that happens, of course. But Mrs. Blair should have considered that fact before she made such ridiculous accusations."

McNeery regarded her shrewdly.

"You can help me a lot if you will."

"How?"

"Induce your father not to sue the Blairs."

"I can't do that."

"Then give up the locket! I won't have my show ruined!"

CHAPTER XXIII

A Startling Surprise

"Mrs. Blair's locket is not in my possession and never has been!" she said coldly. "Please step down from the running-board of my car!"

"Now don't get huffy!" the man pleaded. "I know you hate to confess——"

"There is nothing to confess," Nancy interrupted angrily. "Will you move away from my car?"

"Oh, all right." McNeery fell back reluctantly. "But I'm going over to your father's office and have a talk with him."

The producer found himself speaking into thin air, for Nancy had driven away.

"I certainly am furious!" she said to herself. "How brazen of that man to insinuate that I stole the locket!"

Nancy had intended to pick up her chums, George and Bess, before starting for Crown Point. In her present mood she did not care to see or talk to anyone. However, after driving around the block several times she regained control of her troubled feelings, and betrayed nothing of what was in her mind when she greeted her friends.

They, too, had read the morning papers and were highly indignant at the defaming stories.

"Please, let's not talk about it any more," Nancy pleaded. "I want to forget it if I can."

The girls fell to discussing more cheerful subjects. At first Nancy listened, but soon lost the trend of the conversation. Her attention was attracted to a yellow car which was following close behind her own. When she speeded up it did likewise.

"That's funny," she thought. "I wonder if someone is following me?"

She lost sight of the machine when she turned the next bend. Then, in looking forward to the exciting day they were to spend at Crown Point, she dismissed the matter from her mind.

Fifteen minutes later Nancy felt the steering wheel begin to wobble, and immediately suspected that a tire had gone down. She halted the car and stepped out to look at it.

"It's flat, all right," she informed her friends ruefully.

Before the other two girls could get out to see for themselves, the yellow car that Nancy had noticed earlier pulled up alongside. Abe Jacobs was at the wheel; Francis Clancy beside him. The two men leered triumphantly at the girls.

"Trying to get away, eh?" Jacobs demanded of Nancy.

"Certainly not," the Drew girl returned coldly. "I am on my way to Crown Point."

"A likely story," Jacobs sneered. "You are fleeing over the county line with stolen goods!"

"That's right," Francis chimed in gloatingly. "I'll bet she's got the diamonds in her car now!"

"I most certainly have not," Nancy refuted, stepping back into the automobile and taking her place at the driver's seat. "I tell you I have never seen Mrs. Blair's locket!"

"Colleen said you took it," Francis insisted, "and I'd believe her word before I would yours."

"You might investigate her record!" Nancy said hotly. "You may find a few things that will surprise you."

"Just the same, we'll have a look inside your car," Abe Jacobs drawled, placing his hand on the door handle.

Anger welled up within Nancy at this proposed outrage. She knew that the two men had no right to search her machine and was determined to get away from them even should it mean a ruined tire.

As Jacobs swung open the door, she stepped firmly on the gas pedal. The car spurted forward, and the lawyer was flung backward to the ground.

With a cry of fury Francis Clancy hurled himself upon the running-board of the moving car. Before Nancy was aware of what was happening, he had snapped off the ignition.

"Oh, no you don't!" he sneered.

Abe Jacobs picked himself up from the ground, fuming because he had fallen into a puddle of water.

"You have the diamond locket, Nancy Drew!" he said accusingly. "I'll find it, too!"

He jerked open the car door, and before the girls could make a move to prevent him, he had ripped down the pocket. A hard object instantly thudded to the running-board. It was the diamond locket!

"Ah!" Jacobs cried triumphantly, snatching it up. "We have the thief, Clancy!"

Nancy and her chums were too stunned for the moment to say anything. Who had placed the locket in the car pocket? With sinking hearts they realized that their every act heightened the appearance of their guilt. If they only had not tried to get away!

"I don't know how in the world that locket came to be in my car," Nancy stammered. "I never saw it before in all my life!"

"You can tell that to the judge," Jacobs sneered.

He handed Clancy the diamond trinket.

"This is the one Mrs. Blair lost, isn't it?"

"Sure, this is the one, all right. Colleen told me——"

He broke off quickly, and did not finish his

sentence. Nancy shot a suspicious glance at him. She had not forgotten the conversation she had overheard between Clancy and Colleen the previous day. They had spoken of getting her caught in a police net. How innocently she had walked into their trap!!

"Someone must have put the locket in my car to throw suspicion on me," she defended herself.

"And we have a good idea who it was, too!" George spoke up, glaring at Clancy.

"Miss Drew, you'll have to come back with me to River Heights," Jacobs said sternly. "We have the goods on you this time, and even that smart father of yours won't be able to pull you out of it."

Nancy had no intention of returning to River Heights if she could possibly prevent it, yet she thought it best to appear to give in. She accordingly assumed a dejected pose and said:

"I can't go with you until I get my tire changed."

Back on the road Nancy had caught a glimpse of a car which she knew belonged to a garageman, for it bore the advertisement of his shop in Crown Point. Before Jacobs could protest, she had signaled for the man to stop.

"Can you change my tire for me?" she inquired as he drew up alongside.

"Sure, Miss! That's my business. It won't take me more than ten minutes!"

Jacobs and Clancy were impatient at the delay, but offered no objection to the mechanic fixing the car, since it was impossible for them to take all three of the girls back to River Heights in their coupé. Nancy and her chums alighted, presumably to watch the work.

Jacobs and Clancy lingered about for a time. Then, catching sight of a spring nearby, they wandered over for a drink of water. Nancy had been acting so depressed in spirit that they felt they now had her completely cowed.

This was the opportunity the girl had been seeking. She quickly leaned over and whispered something to the garageman. He looked startled, then nodded.

Bess, by prearrangement, now stole quietly over to Jacobs's parked automobile. Nancy had told her where to find the water cock. She quickly turned it, allowing the contents to drain out upon the ground.

"That should delay things some!" she chuckled.

Nancy ran over to the garageman's automobile and started the motor in an instant. She thrust in the clutch and shot away, while the outraged cries of Clancy and Jacobs rent the air.

The two men ran after the car for a short distance, but realized that they could not hope to overtake it. Nancy had completely outwitted them!

"You let that girl take your car!" Jacobs accused the garageman furiously, as he ran toward his own automobile. "Now what's happened?"

He stared at the stream of water flooding the ground. Before he could reach down to turn the cock, the last drop had drained from the automobile.

"Done again!"

"We can get some water from the spring!" Clancy proposed.

"In what, you fool?"

"You might try carrying it in your hats," the garageman chuckled.

"Don't stand here staring at me!" Jacobs ordered Clancy furiously. "Do something! Find a bucket or even a tin can. We can't run this car without water! We'd burn it up."

While the two men raged, Bess and George quietly returned to Nancy's car as they had been told to do. By this time the mechanic had changed the wheel. Clancy and Jacobs were too excited to notice what the girls were doing.

Suddenly the garageman sprang into Nancy's car. Before the two men could recover from their surprise, they stood watching him drive away with Bess and George.

"I may get into trouble for doing this!" the mechanic chuckled. "But I always like to help a lady in distress! Besides, I didn't care for the looks of those two birds!"

"Where are you taking us?" George inquired curiously.

"The young lady said she'd meet us at my garage in Crown Point. Maybe you've heard of the Skillman Repair Shop. I fix anything that runs on wheels."

Before they reached that place, Bess and George felt very well acquainted with Henry Skillman. They drove up to the garage, and were relieved to see the car which Nancy had taken parked by the gas pump. But the girl herself was nowhere to be seen.

"I guess she must be waiting inside," Bess commented.

The girls found Nancy at the telephone. She had just concluded a long conversation with her father and another with Mrs. Blair. The latter left her somewhat shaken, for the actress showed slight disposition to believe the girl's story about the diamond locket.

"We must get away from here as quickly as we can," Nancy told her companions hurriedly, "or Jacobs and Clancy will be after us in a very short time."

"Yes," George agreed with a laugh, "they'll be hot on the trail as soon as they get their car started. Oh, it was too funny for words to see them so flabbergasted!"

"Before we leave, I want to thank Mr. Skillman for having helped us," Nancy declared.

The garageman was in his shop testing the

punctured tire which had been removed from Nancy's car.

"I was glad to help you out," the man declared.

"Helping ladies is his specialty!" a workman cut in jokingly. "Ask him to tell you how he saved a woman's life about a year ago!"

"I didn't save her life," Skillman growled. "I just picked her up when she was unconscious on the river bank."

"We'd like to hear the story," Nancy declared promptly.

Knowing that they ought to hurry away, Bess and George were surprised that Nancy suddenly had decided to tarry.

"I tell you it wasn't anything," the garageman maintained modestly. "But if you can stand to hear about it, I'll spin the yarn for you girls."

As Nancy and her chums listened, even the former little dreamed of the far-reaching results Mr. Skillman's story was destined to bring about.

CHAPTER XXIV

The Woman in Black

"It was about a year ago," Mr. Skillman began. "I'd been working late at the garage and started home in a pretty bad storm. Just as I came to a bridge over the Muskoka River, a blinding streak of lightning lighted up the sky directly in front of me.

"A terrible clap of thunder followed. For a minute I was stunned, as if I might have been struck."

"You weren't?" Nancy questioned eagerly.

"No. I soon felt all right again and drove on across the bridge. Just then the lightning flashed again. I saw a woman lying along the river bank!"

"She had been struck!" Bess gasped.

"Yes, I thought at first she was dead. Then I worked over her for a while, and after some time she regained her senses enough so that I could get her to a doctor."

"Did she recover?" George asked.

"In a way, yes, but folks say she's never been the same since. She lives alone in a little house over by the cove. Doesn't seem to have any friends and no one knows much about her."

"What is her name?" Nancy asked with bated breath.

"Mrs. Stone."

Nancy looked a trifle disappointed. She had hoped that the woman's initials would tally with those on the locket she had found.

"You don't know her first name, do you?"

"I don't recall that I ever heard it."

"When was it that you aided this woman?"

"About a year ago. In September."

"Do you remember the exact date?"

"Let me think. Why, yes, I do, because my wife went to visit her cousin in Chicago that day. It was September 13th."

Nancy sprang to her feet with an exclamation of pleasure.

"Girls, the dates tally exactly. That old newspaper Enos Crinkle told us about was dated September 13th, too!"

"So it was!" Bess murmured in awe. "Can there be any connection, do you think?"

"I'm sure of it!"

"But the woman's name doesn't correspond to the initials on the locket," George pointed out skeptically.

Nancy refused to be disheartened.

"Stone may not be her real name," she declared. "Perhaps for some reason she changed it. Oh, we must visit the cottage at once!"

"It's easy to find," the garageman directed.

"Just take the river road and turn right when you come to the big bridge."

The girls thanked Mr. Skillman again and raced for the car. As they turned into the side road at the bridge the mechanic had mentioned, Bess glanced back and was startled to see a yellow car following them.

"I believe it's Abe Jacobs!" she exclaimed.

"It looks like his car," George agreed.

Nancy stepped more firmly upon the gas pedal, and they went bouncing over the rough dirt road.

"They're sure to overtake us!" Bess moaned. "We'll all spend the night in jail before they finish with us!"

Nancy had sighted an empty boathouse directly ahead of them. It was wide open. Without an instant's hesitation she drove the car into the shelter. George sprang out to close the doors.

"Driving in here was pure inspiration!" she chuckled. "I guess we've given them the slip again!"

The girls crouched near the window, watching for the approaching automobile. As it came to a halt a short distance from the dilapidated boathouse, they became uneasy. Would the men discover them?

"It's funny. I wonder where that car went all of a sudden!" they heard Jacobs exclaim impatiently. "Believe me, if I ever catch

Nancy Drew I'll make her pay for this wild chase!''

"She must have taken that side road we passed a little way back," Clancy suggested. "We're only losing time to keep on."

To the intense relief of the girls, the men turned their car and drove out of sight.

"Lucky for us they didn't notice the wheel tracks!" Nancy laughed. "Now let's hurry on to the cottage before we have any further delays."

"I noticed a tiny house on the cliff overlooking the river," Bess stated. "That must be the place."

"Probably. We may as well leave the car here and walk," Nancy suggested.

The three girls emerged from the boathouse. Finding a trail leading up the hillside, they followed it to a vine-covered cottage. Their knock brought an elderly servant to the door.

"Mrs. Stone isn't here now," she told the girls.

"When will she be in?" Nancy questioned eagerly. "I must see her."

"She went out for a walk about an hour ago." The woman shook her head sadly. "Poor Mrs. Stone! I feel so sorry for her. And the doctors can't seem to help her at all."

"Has your mistress been ill for some time?" Nancy inquired sympathetically.

"She hasn't been herself since the day of the

accident. You may have heard how it happened. She had crossed the river in a boat and was stepping ashore, when the lightning struck her. She would have died if it hadn't been for a man named Skillman.''

''We were talking to him,'' Nancy explained. ''I feel so sorry for your mistress. I suppose she has many friends to help her.''

The servant shook her head.

''Mrs. Stone is a stranger to Crown Point. I never set eyes on her myself until I came here to work. I've learned to love her, though—she's so sweet and kind. But she's eating her heart out over something and the doctors haven't been able to do anything to help her.''

The girls murmured sympathetically. Presently Nancy asked in what direction Mrs. Stone had gone for her walk.

''Since she's been able to walk out by herself she always chooses the same path along the river.'' The woman indicated a well-beaten trail. ''You can't miss her.''

''Perhaps you had better give us a description of her,'' Nancy suggested.

''She is tall and slender, and has a sweet face—a madonna face, if you know what I mean.''

''Tell me her first name,'' Nancy said, trying to keep her voice steady.

''Sylvia.''

''Sylvia? Oh!''

Bess and George looked at their chum curiously, wondering why she became so startled. Since she as suddenly fell strangely silent, they took it upon themselves to thank the woman for the information.

When the cottage door had closed behind the servant, Nancy wheeled toward her chums, her face aglow.

"Girls, I've solved the mystery at last! I've found the mother of the twins!"

Bess and George regarded her incredulously. They thought that she was taking leave of her senses.

"The date this woman was found is the one before the day on which the twins were picked up," Bess agreed. "I don't see how you can prove any absolute connection among the three, though."

From her pocketbook Nancy removed the two halves of the broken locket. She indicated the initials "S. M. N." on the fragment she had taken from Enos Crinkle's boat.

"The 'S' might stand for Sylvia," George admitted, "but according to my alphabet 'N' doesn't stand for Stone."

"It doesn't need to. You see, I know this woman's real name. I've seen her picture and it tallies with the description her servant gave of her."

"Who is she?" Bess and George cried in one breath.

Nancy did not answer, for already she was running up the path to the water's edge.

"What a revelation it will be if I can convince the poor woman of the truth!" she thought. "I can't get to her too soon!"

Later, Nancy always maintained that at that moment a voice from out of the air whispered to her to make haste. Leaving her chums far behind, she hurriedly climbed the trail leading to the cliff which overlooked the river.

Suddenly Nancy halted. She gasped slightly at what she saw. Far above her, at the edge of a large, flat rock, there knelt a woman in black. Her head was bowed, and she appeared to be in prayer.

Slowly she arose, and with her arms stretched out above her swayed toward the edge of the precipice.

"Wait!" Nancy screamed frantically. "I have news of your babies!"

CHAPTER XXV

NANCY'S TRIUMPH

THE woman in black turned slowly. Nancy, struggling to reach the cliff before it would be too late, thought she had never before seen such a sad, sweet face.

"Wait! Wait!" she cried, almost breathless from running. "I have found your babies!"

A light spread over the woman's face, only to vanish as quickly as it came. She swayed slightly, then sank down upon her knees in a pitiful little heap.

"But they are gone!" she murmured brokenly. "My babies were lost in the storm, and on this very river."

"They floated all night in a boat and were saved," Nancy told her gently. "See, I have the proof."

From her pocketbook she took the two halves of the heart-shaped locket.

"My locket!" the woman exclaimed. "Where did you find it?"

"It was picked up near the babies. You are Sylvia McNeery, are you not?"

"Yes! Yes!" the woman cried, almost beside herself with excitement. "Oh, who are you? And are you certain the babies are mine?"

By this time Bess and George had come up, puffing from the strenuous climb, and the three girls introduced themselves. They confirmed Nancy's story about finding the locket in the same boat with the twins. As the woman stared at the broken trinket, she gradually became convinced of the truth of what Nancy had told her.

"Oh, where are my darling babies?" she cried joyfully. "Take me to them!"

Nancy and her chums soothed Mrs. McNeery as well as they could. After they had calmed her somewhat, they led her back to the cottage.

"We will bring your babies to you within an hour," Nancy promised. "You must not excite yourself."

"I haven't seen my darling twins for a year," the woman sobbed happily. "Until you told me they were alive and well, Miss Drew, I didn't want to go on living."

"You have a great deal to live for now," Nancy assured her gently. "Your husband wants you back, too."

"Edwin wants me to come home?" the woman stammered.

"Yes, he told me so himself."

"But he doesn't like babies—and I can't give up the twins."

After Mrs. McNeery had rested a few moments, she declared that she was strong enough for the drive to River Heights in Nancy's automobile. Feeling that the suspense of waiting might do the poor mother more harm than the ride, the girls decided after a brief consultation to take her with them to the Drew home.

Before leaving Crown Point, Nancy telephoned her father and likewise Miss Brown, asking the latter to bring Jay and Janet to River Heights without delay.

"I'll do it even if it costs me my position," the nurse promised. "Mr. and Mrs. Blair are having a terrible argument in the library. It has something to do with their contracts!"

During the drive to River Heights, Mrs. McNeery told Nancy of her past. At the height of her career as an actress she had determined to give up the stage forever, and devote herself exclusively to her babies. When her husband, who put business ahead of everything else, had threatened to take them from her, she had slipped away. Carrying them in her arms, she had floated down the Muskoka River in a boat she had found tied up along the shore.

"I was half insane with grief," the actress explained. "I didn't know what I was doing. I remember that a storm came up and that I tried to land the boat. I had just stepped out upon shore when everything went black and I

knew no more. When I recovered consciousness, I found that my babies were gone. Whenever I cried for them, the doctors said I had
lost my mind.''

"Don't think about it any more," Nancy
comforted. "Everything will be all right
now, I'm sure.''

Desperately Nancy hoped that all would be
well. She did not distress Mrs. McNeery by
telling her that the babies had been adopted by
the Blairs, however.

"If Kitty Blair refuses to give them up, I
don't know how things can be righted," she
thought. "Perhaps Father can find a way out,
though.''

When Nancy drove up in front of her own
home a few minutes later, Hannah came rush-
ing out to meet her.

"Miss Brown is here, and she has the twins
with her! Nancy Drew, if you've brought
them here to live, after promising me——''

"You needn't worry, Hannah," Nancy
laughed. "From this day on the babies shall
be cared for by their own mother!''

She then introduced Mrs. McNeery to the
flustered housekeeper. Recovering from her
first surprise, Hannah invited everyone into the
house.

Nancy never quite forgot the happy scene
which was enacted in the living room. Sylvia
McNeery sobbed with joy as she clasped her

babies in her arms. She was not content until
Miss Brown had told her every detail of how
the twins had been found in the boat.

"I know how you must feel about giving up
the twins twice after you have looked upon
them as your own charges," Mrs. McNeery said
kindly to the nurse. "I should be very happy
if you would consent to enter my employ. I
must find someone to assist me with the babies, and I could never secure a nurse who
would love them as you do."

Miss Brown's face lighted with joy.

"Oh, Mrs. McNeery," she murmured gratefully. "I do love the babies, and I'd like nothing better than to look after them always!"

The day was filled with surprises. A few
minutes later Carson Drew entered the house
accompanied by Edwin McNeery. The producer seemed changed—more subdued, Nancy
observed.

"Where is Sylvia—my wife?" he asked
tensely.

Nancy led him to the living room. For an
awkward moment Mrs. McNeery and her husband stared at each other; then the theatrical
man went over to his wife.

"Sylvia, I've searched everywhere for you.
I want you back home again."

"And the babies?" she whispered.

McNeery did not flinch at the question.

"Of course you shall stay with them!" he

said heartily. ''I've been selfish and mean, but from now on I'm going to be different. Stay at home with the children. I'll never ask you again to be an actress.''

As McNeery drew his wife into his arms, Nancy and her friends quietly stole away. They noticed Carson Drew looked somewhat troubled, and questioned him. He admitted that he was worrying about the adoption papers the Blairs had signed.

''Oh, everything is working out so beautifully,'' Nancy declared. ''It will be terrible if Kitty and Johnny ruin things by refusing to give up the babies.''

''We'll ask them to come here and find out what they have to say,'' Mr. Drew proposed.

The Blairs arrived at the house half an hour later. It was obvious from their manner that something had gone decidedly wrong. Nancy was quite bewildered when the actor and actress refused to set foot in the living room until Edwin McNeery had left. This he obligingly did for them.

''What is the matter?'' Nancy questioned them curiously.

''My career has been ruined!'' Kitty stormed. ''And by McNeery, too! Oh, I hope I shall never see him again.''

Gradually Nancy became acquainted with the fact that the Blairs had failed to live up to a clause in the contract they had signed, to the effect that if they should fail to attend rehearsals they would break the agreement. They had not appeared at a practice set for three o'clock that afternoon. Tried beyond endurance, McNeery had telephoned them that he was abandoning the show and that they were discharged.

"He tore up our contracts!" Kitty cried furiously. "I think I'll sue him!"

"I'm afraid you'll not win your case," Mr. Drew smiled.

"I can't bear to live near River Heights another day," the actress wailed. "Johnny, you must take me on a long cruise around the world."

"But, my dear, we have no money for such a trip," Johnny remonstrated. "My creditors give me no peace now!"

It was some time before Nancy could bring up the subject of the twins. When she did so, Kitty showed slight disposition to discuss them. She was not even interested in Nancy's statement that she knew a woman who claimed to be the real mother.

"I always felt that if the mother of those babies should turn up I'd be ruined," she declared superstitiously. "I never want to see the woman!"

"We've had nothing but bad luck since the day we adopted the twins," Johnny growled.

"I hope taking them with you on your cruise

won't spoil the trip for you," Nancy commented adroitly.

"Take them with us!" Kitty screamed. "Well, I guess we won't! I've had enough of children for the rest of my life."

"Then you mean you want to give them up?" Nancy asked quickly.

"Take them back to the Home, for all I care! Or give them to that woman who claims they're her own. I don't care what becomes of them!"

Mr. Drew thrust a paper before her, indicating the line where she was to write her name. Without stopping to read the printed matter, Mrs. Blair signed away all rights to the twins. She looked relieved as she turned to go.

"Oh, Miss Drew, about that diamond necklace of mine—I guess I was mistaken."

"Then you know that I did not take it!" Nancy exclaimed eagerly. "How did you find it out?"

"This afternoon Abe Jacobs telephoned me that he had recovered the locket and that Francis Clancy would bring it to the house. But I never got it. I just learned that Colleen and Clancy eloped, taking my diamonds with them! I now know that Colleen told me lies about you in order to divert suspicion from herself."

Before Nancy could express relief at being cleared of all implication in the theft, Mrs. Blair and her husband swept from the house.

Nancy and her friends never saw the couple again. A few days later it became generally known that the Blairs had left town hurriedly to avoid their many creditors.

Reunited with her husband, and happy to have the babies again, Mrs. McNeery seemed like a new woman. Her face glowed as with an inner light. She looked younger and very happy.

Mr. and Mrs. McNeery found words inadequate in telling Nancy of their appreciation for what she had done for them. They planned to purchase a palatial country home near River Heights. Rodney Brown was to be their chauffeur.

"We owe everything to you, Miss Drew," Rodney said to Nancy later that day in a voice that trembled with emotion. "I think you are the most remarkable person I have ever met."

Nancy had been worried for fear that Abe Jacobs's story had hurt her reputation. However, the entire matter was explained and published prominently in all the evening papers. Any insinuations against Nancy were retracted, and she was cleared of all suspicion. Incidentally, Carson Drew later dropped his suit against Jacobs, as he felt that the man's ostracism by the community was sufficient punishment.

As was to be expected, Nancy received more praise than can be imagined for the clever manner in which she had traced the parentage of the twin babies, and in uniting the other pair of twins, Ruth and Rodney. The newspapers carried headlines of the story, as well as the pictures of all involved therein. That evening the telephone rang continually, bringing personal messages of congratulation from admirers and well-wishers.

Late that night, tired but happy over her triumph, Nancy slipped into her father's study where he sat in his lounging robe, dreamily blowing rings of smoke toward the ceiling and watching them dissolve into formless vapor. She snuggled down in the big lounge chair beside him and rested her head on his shoulder. The two gazed into the open fire before them.

"When I look into those flames," remarked Nancy, "I am reminded of other fireplaces. Wasn't it strange how broken lockets and broken hearts went together?"

"And stranger still, how you managed to reunite the two, and make so many people happy," praised her father.

THE END

THE NANCY DREW MYSTERY STORIES
By CAROLYN KEENE

Illustrated. Every Volume Complete in Itself.

Here is a thrilling series of mystery stories for girls. Nancy Drew, ingenious, alert, is the daughter of a famous criminal lawyer and she herself is deeply interested in his mystery cases. Her interest involves her often in some very dangerous and exciting situations.

THE SECRET OF THE OLD CLOCK
Nancy, unaided, seeks to locate a missing will and finds herself in the midst of adventure.

THE HIDDEN STAIRCASE
Myterious happenings in an old stone mansion lead to an investigation by Nancy.

THE BUNGALOW MYSTERY
Nancy has some perilous experiences around a deserted bungalow.

THE MYSTERY AT LILAC INN
Quick thinking and quick action were needed for Nancy to extricate herself from a dangerous situation.

THE SECRET AT SHADOW RANCH
On a vacation in Arizona Nancy uncovers an old mystery and solves it.

THE SECRET OF RED GATE FARM
Nancy exposes the doings of a secret society on an isolated farm.

THE CLUE IN THE DIARY
A fascinating and exciting story of a search for a clue to a surprising mystery.

NANCY'S MYSTERIOUS LETTER
Nancy receives a letter informing her that she is heir to a fortune. This story tells of her search for another Nancy Drew.

THE SIGN OF THE TWISTED CANDLES
Nancy, as mediator in a generation-old feud, divulges an unknown birthright.

THE PASSWORD TO LARKSPUR LANE
A carrier pigeon furnishes Nancy with a clue to a mysterious retreat.

GROSSET & DUNLAP, Publishers, NEW YORK